FILM STARS

Stars are an integral part of every major film industry in the world.
In this pivotal new series, each book is devoted to an international
movie star, looking at the development of their identity, their acting
and performance methods, the cultural significance of their work,
and their influence and legacy. Taking a wide range of different stars,
including George Clooney, Brigitte Bardot, and Dirk Bogarde amongst
others, this series encompasses the sphere of silent and sound acting,
Hollywood and non-Hollywood areas of cinema, and child and adult
forms of stardom. With its broad range, but a focus throughout on
the national and historical dimensions to film, the series offers
students and researchers a new approach to studying film.

SERIES EDITORS
Martin Shingler and Susan Smith

PUBLISHED TITLES
Brigitte Bardot *Ginette Vincendeau*
Carmen Miranda *Lisa Shaw*
Elizabeth Taylor *Susan Smith*
Nicole Kidman *Pam Cook*
Star Studies: A Critical Guide *Martin Shingler*

FORTHCOMING
Mickey Rourke *Keri Walsh*

Barbara **STANWYCK**

ANDREW KLEVAN

palgrave
macmillan

A BFI book published by Palgrave Macmillan

Dedicated to Mr. Alan Kelk and his English Literature lessons in
Broomefield, Cheadle Hulme School

First published in 2013 by
PALGRAVE MACMILLAN

on behalf of the

BRITISH FILM INSTITUTE
21 Stephen Street, London W1T 1LN
www.bfi.org.uk

There's more to discover about film and television through the BFI. Our world-renowned archive,
cinemas, festivals, films, publications and learning resources are here to inspire you.

Palgrave Macmillan in the UK is an imprint of Macmillan Publishers Limited, registered
in England, company number 785998, of Houndmills, Basingstoke, Hampshire RG21 6XS.
Palgrave Macmillan in the US is a division of St Martin's Press LLC, 175 Fifth Avenue, New
York, NY 10010. Palgrave Macmillan is the global academic imprint of the above companies and
has companies and representatives throughout the world. Palgrave® and Macmillan® are
registered trademarks in the United States, the United Kingdom, Europe and other countries.

Designed by couch
Cover images: (front) *Stella Dallas* (King Vidor, 1937), Samuel Goldwyn, Inc.; (back) *The Lady Eve*
(Preston Sturges, 1941), © Paramount Productions

Set by Cambrian Typesetters, Camberley, Surrey
Printed in China

This book is printed on paper suitable for recycling and made from fully managed and sustained
forest sources. Logging, pulping and manufacturing processes are expected to conform to the
environmental regulations of the country of origin.

British Library Cataloguing-in-Publication Data
A catalogue record for this book is available from the British Library
A catalog record for this book is available from the Library of Congress

ISBN 978–1–84457–648–7 (pb)

CONTENTS

ACKNOWLEDGMENTS

I would like to thank Martin Shingler and Susan Smith for inviting me to contribute to their handsome series of monographs. Thank you also for allowing me to choose my preferred performer and pursue my approach. Thank you to the University of Oxford and St Anne's College for granting me study leave to write the book. Thank you to all the intelligent students over many years who have enthusiastically joined with me in opening up the films. My exchanges with V.F. Perkins continue to help my work. Alex Clayton, Edward Gallafent, Steven Peacock, Joanna Penglase, Vivienne Penglase, Douglas Pye and Susan Smith all read a complete draft of the manuscript and made invaluable comments, corrections and suggestions. The book is now better than it would have been, and I am very grateful to them. I am indebted to Vivienne for her love and support (though she is too generous to accept that I owe her anything). Cassandra and Chomsky, my cats, kept me company throughout the days – even after I had fed them. Barbara Stanwyck's performances were a constant inspiration. I hope the book does them justice.

INTRODUCTION

One of the greatest actresses I ever worked with.

Walter Huston

[Howard Hawks] always ranked her among the best actresses with whom he ever worked.

Hawks biographer Todd McCarthy

A fantastic actress.

Mitchell Leisen

A professional's professional, a superb technician.

King Vidor

An instinct so sure she almost needed no direction.

Preston Sturges

Stanwyck, of course, was a brilliant actress. She could do anything.

William Wellman

(Nehme 2007)

The aim of this study is to show why Barbara Stanwyck justifies this praise. To fulfil this aim, it examines her performances in nine Hollywood films. This is only a fraction of a huge body of work spanning many decades. Born in Brooklyn, New York City, in 1907, she appeared in over eighty theatrical features and many television episodes from 1927 to 1985 (the exact facts vary slightly from source to source). Biographies of her already exist (DiOrio 1984; Madsen 2001; Wayne 2009) as do studies that combine biography with film commentary (Smith 1974; Callahan 2012). The books by Ella Smith and Dan Callahan provide a discussion, one by one, of each of her films. Although her book is partly aimed at coffee tables, Smith has a good eye for picking out key moments and aspects of technique. It is also worthwhile for its extensive provision of quotation from Stanwyck's collaborators and a splendid array of stills. Callahan's recent study ambitiously merges biographical knowledge with a spirited assessment of her films, and is full of alert and agile observation and forthright judgement. Readers wishing to receive a more comprehensive overview of her life and work may wish to consult these books.

Another approach was necessary in order not to replicate, and for a study more compact. There are many books of criticism that use 'close reading' to analyse, interpret and celebrate the style of a director (and which rarely call on biography). There are far fewer dedicated to individual star performers. The present study concentrates on evaluating the style and meaning of Barbara Stanwyck's performances. It homes in on a selection of her exemplary films and scenes to highlight the detail of her performances, and to recognise moment-by-moment dynamics and tensions.

The book divides into five chapters, each one devoted to a quality of Stanwyck's performances: responsiveness, multiplicity, tonal finesse, restraint and stillness. These qualities are foregrounded to explore, and stress, Stanwyck's distinction, but they should also be of interest to the study of performance more generally, and to film criticism and appreciation. Although I have endeavoured to make the format not too insistently determining, it has the advantage of providing a series of conceptual anchors – each chapter orbiting around its respective quality – something the film-by-film arrangement does not as readily permit. The chapters are also divided generically (or categorically) and proceed chronologically to show how each quality intersects with material across her career:

pre-Code (early 1930s), early melodrama (late 1930s), comedy (early 1940s), thriller/film noir (mid 1940s), and late melodrama (1950s). Although each quality is coupled with the genre or category in which it is most revelatory, the implication is that each will be found elsewhere (for example, in her Westerns which are not discussed), but not everywhere, in her work. More specifically, the first chapter performs a general, introductory role assessing some prevalent characteristics of her style and persona.

The study also offers a renewed opportunity to assess characteristics attributed to her films. Many of them are established classics of Hollywood cinema's 'Golden Age', regularly, and frequently, analysed inside and outside of the academy. Callahan's book, aside from the odd reference, neither explicitly nor implicitly recognises the decades of commentary. Given the range of commentary on her films – such as on *Stella Dallas* (1937) whose meaning has long been a matter of dispute – there was a place for a less segregated account. Furthermore, my viewings – not simply those during this book's preparation but over many years of teaching the films – were bound up inextricably with the commentaries, and my assessments have adapted in response to their interpretations and evaluations. It is in this way that interpretive and evaluative contexts are as valuable as historical, cultural and biographical ones.

The body of interpretation is also useful for this study because as well as wishing to highlight the details of performance it is equally interested in how the performer relates to the wider concerns of a film (and the concerns of the film-makers), and how she might convey or adjust them. The purpose of dedicating longer chapters to individual films – Chapter Two on *Stella Dallas* and Chapter Four on *Double Indemnity* (1944) – is to examine Stanwyck's performance within the context of a whole film, rather than one or two quintessential sequences. It is also to work through, more systematically, her relationship to the variety and depth of meaning as proposed by the commentaries. Some of her films have become models in Film Studies, so this presents an opportunity to revisit classic topics of the discipline such as female roles and representation (e.g. the 'sacrificial mother' or the 'femme fatale'), psychoanalysis, medium reflexivity and Sirkian irony, and to examine them in relation to her performances. One intention is to see how a range of different, even apparently divergent, perspectives may be brought together. Another is to make these perspectives accessible to those unfamiliar with them, such as students and non-academic readers, in accord with the pedagogical remit of the series. I hope I engage in fair and patient conversation with representative quotation, but there is critique. The chapter on *Stella Dallas* shows that, although the many different interpretations of the film are enabled by Stanwyck's multi-faceted performance, she defeats the more adamant claims. The chapter on *Double Indemnity* argues that the description of Stanwyck's character as an evil 'femme fatale' insufficiently recognises the qualities of her portrayal. Focusing on the central performer, as well as endorsing and enhancing familiar understandings, permits us to think again, and provides fresh illumination.

Not all that is significant in a film can be attributed to a performer, of course, and the essential role of other creative personnel, especially the director, means that not all that is significant about a performance can be attributed to the skill of a performer. The study is concerned to recognise Stanwyck's skills but it is also interested in the presentation of her, and her characters, by the film. It suggests how Stanwyck's performances interrelate with the world of the film as created by others. Although specific individuals with whom she collaborated are acknowledged, when I refer to 'the film' in the text, attributing to it an agency, I mean to imply all that is involved in its creation. Symbiosis troubles attribution – the question of who influences who remains indefinite – and, even when I ascribe qualities and achievements to her, the implication is not that she is the sole creator or inventor of them. At the same time, one does not want to undervalue her as a core participant, and there is much to be gained from attending to the presence and execution of Barbara Stanwyck.

1 RESPONSIVENESS

LADIES OF LEISURE (1930)
THE MIRACLE WOMAN (1931)
NIGHT NURSE (1931)

Independence is a trait commonly attributed to the Barbara Stanwyck film persona. In his classic text, *Stars*, Richard Dyer mentions her within a section entitled 'The Independent Woman' (1998 [1979]: 54–9), and David Thomson in his entry in *A Biographical Dictionary of Film* writes, 'There is not a more credible portrait in the cinema of a worldly, attractive, and independent woman in a man's world than Stanwyck's career revealed' (1995 [1975]: 712). This independence is noticeable even in her first appearance in her first significant film *Ladies of Leisure* (1930) (she appeared without credit as a dancer in 1927, and then in two unsuccessful films in 1929). It is the middle of the night, we are watching from the road, and she appears in the distance, beyond a stretch of water, arriving at a jetty in a rowing boat. When Jerry Strong (Ralph Graves) calls out to her and offers help, she says that he can – by looking the other way. She is a tiny figure in the frame, but we can see her kicking the boat away and standing on the jetty in a white evening dress, with her hands on her hips. Jerry looks round and warns that she will lose the boat but she shouts back (only faintly audible on the old print I am watching) 'I wanna lose it. It ain't mine'. Then she struts hastily around the jetty, and strides up a grassy verge to meet him. Her independence is established in a minute or so: her isolation (alone on a boat in the middle of night), her distance (from the camera), her self-sufficiency, her determination, her incongruity, her physicality, her stance, her defiance, her disregard, and her call for privacy.

Other aspects of the Stanwyck persona, much remarked upon, and associated with independence, are also in evidence in the opening few minutes: the 'tough cookie', 'no-nonsense' girl from the streets who has 'been around' and knows her mind. She speaks in Brooklynese, jaunty and raucous with elongated vowels, a bit sharp at the top of the range, and slangy with lots of 'say … .', 'hey', 'oughta', 'oh gee', 'oh boy' and 'sure' (pronounced '*shaaw*'). Her behaviour is 'unladylike': she freely gesticulates, for example, thumbing over to the ship on the water, vigorously squeezes her nose with his handkerchief before giving a sniff, and wiggles her bottom to get comfy as she sits in the car. It transpires that being a 'party girl' is her 'racket', and that she has sneaked out from a large disreputable party on a ship. 'Party girl' is a euphemism for the already euphemistic 'call girl' and a useful one for Hollywood to suggest illicit conduct in the guise of vivacity and merriment. Given, as she says, that it is '4 in the *ay-em*', and that she has just been on a rowing boat, it is little wonder that her hair is bedraggled, her eye makeup has run, and one shoulder strap on her dress has snapped. At the same time, the film insinuates unfettered behaviour and manhandling.

Apart from providing the erotic whiff of clandestine and 'immoral' sex, by making Kay Arnold, Stanwyck's character, a 'call girl', she is provided with a reason to be direct *and* indirect: the straight-talking, forthright girl who, nevertheless, cannot or will not always say it like it is. Stanwyck's best characters often have a reason to be deceitful, a pretext enabling her to control the release of truth. Many good film performers explore and complicate the relationship between authenticity and artifice, a tension that is itself at the heart of the medium (with its equal propensities to record and design), or merge their performance with their character's performances within the fiction. Yet, sincerity, in particular, is often at stake in Stanwyck's performances. Dan Callahan describes her as 'an actress who always makes "sincerity" seem a Byzantine concept' (2012: 150). (The *performing* of sincerity is itself an intriguing paradox.) Kay's jaunty explanation of her job to Jerry is as euphemistic as 'party girl' – 'if you need a girl, I'm the one you call for, I'm the filler in' – but is delivered as handy and helpful, an advertising slogan innocently appropriated. A few moments later, she secretly discovers Jerry's fat wallet (he's wealthy) in the inside pocket of his coat, and, after registering the import with a serious face, she breezily exclaims, 'Lovely night, isn't it?' Her job requires her to create amenable environments (for men) without appearing to do so, while the prospect of pecuniary gain enhances the night's loveliness for her, and Stanwyck's exclamation conveys a little of both. Yet, her delivery of the line is not decisively cynical or dissembling, nor is it said with avaricious relish. The night *really* does now appear to Kay as lovely, and it matters that it does.

Frank Capra's films show a director who was also interested in exploring the expression of sincerity. He made four with Stanwyck in the early 1930s (*Ladies of Leisure, The Miracle Woman, Forbidden, The Bitter Tea of General Yen*, all between 1930 and 1933). The appreciation of Capra's later films has tended to overshadow this earlier work and the significance of his partnership with Stanwyck, but the recent interest in the pre-Code period of Hollywood (1930–4) has helped the rediscovery. Richard T. Jameson writes that, 'viewed as collaborations between a gutsy star and gutsy director at a crucially formative stage in their careers, and in the sound cinema as well, all four films are extraordinarily exciting – indeed, almost indecently electrifying' (1981: 37). Joseph McBride writes, 'The intensity and lucidity of their work together ... is one of the most fertile creative teamings of director and actress in cinema history' (2010: 47).

Important though Stanwyck's characters' independence may be, the description possibly overlooks their willingness to interact. They are rarely detached or aloof (even *Double Indemnity*'s restrained

Phyllis Dietrichson [1944]), and are mostly eager to engage. When Jerry says he *too* has ducked out of a party (which he has), Kay squirms in glee at the coincidence. She is restrained only by the realisation that her dress strap has fallen away, which forces her into a self-conscious and contrite pardon. He says it serves her right for attending *that* type of party, and she snaps indignantly at his self-righteousness ('Heh, if ya gonna preach, I'll *waahlk*'). Despite their diversity and proximity, each of these – the gleeful squirm, the self-conscious pardon, the indignant snap – is a striking, full-blooded reaction to which Kay (and Stanwyck) is equally committed. As Mick LaSalle writes, 'Stanwyck inhabited [a] wide ... emotional range ... and she could access any of her emotions at a moment's notice ... with no inconsistency of character' (2000: 136). Range, quite rightly, is commonly attributed to the performer, prompting Anthony Lane to describe her as the 'Swiss Army knife of motion pictures. She could be used for anything – fighting, dancing, weeping, wailing, cracking wise' (2007). Range and responsiveness go hand in hand: responding wholeheartedly to different activities, circumstances and people requires range. The achievement of range is especially impressive in Stanwyck's case because she was not a character actor of the type who adopts a variety of conspicuous façades from film to film.

In *Ladies of Leisure*, her flexibility (of response) is contrasted with rigidity; inflexibility is a theme of the film, and a structuring feature. Convinced that she represents Hope, Jerry, an amateur painter (and not a particularly good one, judging by what we glimpse of his work), turns her into his model. Artists' models were a favourite signifier of scandal in Hollywood's pre-Code films (LaSalle: 83), but while friends and family see only disgrace, Jerry's intentions are high-minded. Much of the film concerns Kay trying to break free of the static and restrictive poses she must adopt for the portraiture and – attracted by his lack of *moves* and social graces – getting him to notice her. Jerry is a stiff, unresponsive figure, the first in a long line of stolid leading men that Stanwyck would play against or, as Stephen Harvey wickedly describes them, 'globs of unleavened dough' (1981: 36). Even Fred MacMurray, a deceptively agile performer (and with whom she made a number of her best films), has a thickset frame, bulky, rectangular face and solid demeanour. While she spends her time alertly responding to their characters, they often fail to regard hers satisfactorily. Her lively receptivity is set against their insensitivity, the consequences of which vary depending on the genre.

Often the male performers are in control of their limitations, but in *Ladies of Leisure*, as Jameson writes, '[Ralph] Graves ... an awkwardly grinning Varsity jock ... comes across as a staggeringly unpolished player who scarcely knows what line-reading, let alone acting, is about. He earnestly wants to get it right, but more than once he starts to speak before he's been given his proper cue; he waits good-naturedly for the other fellow to conclude his business, then proceeds as if no great harm had been done ... this is coping, not deliberate stylization' (38). Either way, this quality in her leading men provides a dramatic test for Stanwyck, one that might be less testing were she a performer (happy to be) left to her own devices. In his book 'Star Acting', Charles Affron compellingly examines Lillian Gish, Greta Garbo, and Bette Davis and argues that they have a plastic, malleable expressivity that borders on the fantastic (1977). Although they respond intensely to their surroundings, they then produce patterns of performance which are self-generating and self-justifying. In contrast, the performer who modulates and calibrates her response to other characters (and performers) is challenged to sustain interest in less flamboyant ways. Stanwyck, even when she is performing extreme aspects of character, keeps herself within reach, and maintains a manner that may be reciprocated. Many of the great female film performers endow their characters with distinctive, eloquent and complex responses to the failure of others to acknowledge them (Cavell: 1996). Stanwyck, however, seems to be the performer who, despite the obstacles, explores ways in which one might acknowledge others.

Graves's performance is not the only stilted feature of *Ladies of Leisure*. As Jameson writes, 'The stage origins remain conspicuous in much of the shooting ... [and] [t]heatrical types dominate the supporting characterizations and, for that matter, the casting' (37). Add to this the limitations on mobility faced by early sound films, and Pauline Kael is fair when she describes it as 'a museum piece'. At the same time, for Kael, the archaic environment 'emphasizes Stanwyck's remarkable modernism' (1993 [1982]: 403). The 'modernism' to which Kael refers might be Stanwyck's lucid and undemonstrative naturalism that trusts to the camera's observational power. Jerry is finding Kay a cigarette and something with which to light it, and this takes enough time to create a little in-between period as she waits. It is their first interaction on meeting and the first time we are close enough to see her face. Kay's expressions are light,

brief, and incomplete: her eyes follow his movements, the side of her mouth tightens and upturns a touch self-consciously, and she purses her lips before taking the cigarette. Her behaviour suggests, very faintly, something stirred or stirring – her eyes, for example, not simply watching but noticing – and yet, at the same time, it looks unexceptional, in keeping with the delay, and the awkwardness of strangers meeting. Stanwyck is capable of small and large-scale effects, but Terrence Rafferty captures the former well when he writes, 'Her effects are small-scale, plain: a downturn at the corners of her mouth, a sudden softening in the tone of her voice, a flicker of self-doubt in her eyes. Such nearly imperceptible but always perfectly lucid shifts of emphasis were her basic arsenal of technical firepower' (2007).

Her flexibility extends to the performance of extraneous actions. A cigarette painfully sticks to the skin of her lower lip and she fretfully stutters 'agh, agh, agh'. Kay's personality is revealed through an occurrence that is incidental and passing (indeed, it takes place whilst lighting one cigarette with another and passing it across to him). This flexibility includes idiosyncrasy. Buoyed by the thick wallet and the 'lovely night', she turns to him while he drives and sucks in her cheeks (as if she were impersonating a fish), and asks him whether he can do the same. Later, she starts posing for him in his apartment, where most of the action takes place, and he is exasperated that she cannot be what *he* wants her to be (he says, 'I want you to be yourself', to which she replies 'then what the devil are you trying to change me for?'). Jerry rubs off her makeup and strips away her fake eyelashes (she lets out the strangest melodic yelp, like the sound of a small animal), exclaiming that he wants to see the 'real' her while at the same time demanding that she look up, see through the ceiling, imagine the sky, and appear as a vision of Hope! In response, Kay bursts out 'goody – goody – goody – let's fight', opens her hands in front of her chest, and then says 'boom' as her fist meets her palm. Performed with childish glee, but speeded up and softened to give her exclamation a miniature and parodic form, it marks a sudden shift in tenor and tone. It is cheerfully surprising not simply as an impulsive piece of behaviour by Kay but as an unpredictable form of acting by Stanwyck. The idiosyncrasy of character is matched by that of performance, for just as Kay will not conform (to Jerry's demands), Stanwyck does not conform to a particular acting style or method.

The detail and light touch of Stanwyck's performance works in response to the starchy and stagy environment, not simply in spite of it. To tease him, Kay does a number of mocking impersonations of female stereotypes (girlish, adoring, coy), in the same vibrant and playful, but hemmed-in, style of the 'goody, goody' outburst. Most of them take place at some distance from the camera. Perhaps because it is an early sound film, the recording technology is not supportive, and there is a sense, even when the camera is relatively close to Stanwyck, of her being left, bereft, to draw our attention by herself. In Manny Farber's terms, this would be a 'termite' performance, intricate and concise, proceeding with an honest, unpretentious vitality (2009 [1962]). Stanwyck may well be nibbling away at the wooden world of the film, but she reacts to what is at hand, and is not dispirited. She treats unprepossessing material in good faith, and the less than conducive context makes her treatment unexpectedly touching, and generous.

Stanwyck is not only responsive to other actors but to latent intensities in the material. She finds distinct ways of realising the script (even if screenwriter or director guided her). Bill Standish (Lowell Sherman), the drunken womaniser, is coming on to Kay when he asks, 'Done any posing before?', to which she replies, smiling while pushing her hair under her hat in the mirror, 'I'm always posing'. He follows up with 'How do you spend your nights?' and she replies '*Re*posing!' This retort is already succinctly witty, and an actor, and the film, could be forgiven for making sure the timing is right and letting the line punch for itself. Stanwyck does something more. Leaving the mirror, Kay comes right up to Standish, leans against the wall, cocks her head towards him, beams a large smile, and then, on finishing the word 'reposing', flicks her head straight. This straightening of the head, as she puts him straight, is confident but not too cocky. Her rebuff is almost warm-hearted, while pointedly putting an end to the matter. She does not take the more obvious opportunities presented in the dialogue to stand back, dry and aloof, nor does she lay on the sass, sardonic and sly. She approaches him, stands face to face, and addresses him directly. This is how she keeps her distance. Moreover, her response is appropriate – after all, this unhappy alcoholic is easily brushed aside and hardly requires ferocity – but equally it sets the standards for appropriateness, teaching us how to treat him. We learn about, assess, or reconsider character(s) thanks to the precise nature of her regard (for example, her behaviour with Jerry delivers a fuller account of him than Graves is capable of revealing).

Stanwyck's characters can be audaciously forthright. This is forcefully exhibited in the opening scene of *The Miracle Woman* (1931), another of her films with Frank Capra, where she plays Florence Fallon, a preacher and faith healer. Florence walks out in front of a church congregation to read a sermon written by her father. Within a minute or so, she is delivering a searing critique of the congregation's callousness. (Her father wanted to stay on as pastor until he died as reward for his devoted years of service, but was shunted aside in favour of a younger man.) As an occasion of passionate, public exhortation, in the context of losing innocence and finding a voice, it joins hands with those that appear in other Capra films (most notably, *Mr Smith Goes to Washington* [1939]). The scene is equally commanding but the achievement is more unusual. This is because it has a woman providing the persuasive rhetoric; because it initiates rather than culminates, so the ground has not been prepared to substantiate the outpouring and channel the sentiment; and because, less framed and nurtured as a set piece, it has a raw immediacy. Stanwyck is exposed, and she generates intensity and conviction with few of the customary mechanisms of support.

Florence begins by reading her father's sermon hesitantly and inexpressively. Then she says, 'you have seen fit to call another, a younger man to guide and serve you', slowing her speech on 'guide and serve you', looking up from her text and flicking her eyes around the congregants accusingly. We see the first buds of rhetoric and exhibition but, crucially, her techniques of oratory are born out of a sincere anger towards the congregation. By the time she says, 'Woe unto you hypocrites', we are firmly in hell-fire preacher territory, but the familiar expressions of outrage emerge from what appears as an honest accusation. Any future fakery in her role as faith healer is complicated by the integrity of the origins. The line between sincerity and deceit is blurred in many Stanwyck roles but *The Miracle Woman* does not simply present a fully formed character that will represent the blurring. It provides the scene of initiation. When Florence starts shouting at the congregation, she is also breaking into tears and her voice is cracking, so uncontrollable distress conjoins with oratory and projection. She is immersed in a church environment and knows its teachings by heart: in a world where the spiritual is already bound up with the theatrical, scriptures slip into script.

Charles Affron argues that Capra's films are powered by persuasive voices and 'political, social and ethical systems' are explored through the dynamism of voices within, and across, spaces (in this film, the church, the tabernacle, the apartment block). Spaces are discovered and given dimension not simply by the camera but by the direction and flow of voices. For Affron, Capra has an 'ethos of vocality' and his films are located in 'vocal melody' as much as they are in images. (1982: 116–18). Florence's fearlessness is exemplified by her brazen confrontation with the figure of the Deacon, sitting in the congregation, played by Charles Middleton – later to incarnate the villain Ming in the Flash Gordon serials – and she is not terrified, as most of us are, by his reverberating, *merciless*, incantatory voice. Pointing at him, and then the stained glass window of Christ, she shouts out: 'My father is dead ... You crucified him'. The Deacon reprimands her, 'You are in a house of God', to which she replies, '*What God? Whose God – yours?* – this isn't a house of God – this is a meeting place for hypocrites', and by now she is yelling, her voice testing the limits of the soundtrack. LaSalle writes: 'For scorching, burning, blinding fury we must turn to ... Barbara Stanwyck ... she could erupt ... into blind hysteria – into tear-spraying, drool-spitting, shrieking, racking wrath. In almost every one of her pre-Codes, there is a moment when that wire gets tripped and the floodgates open'. LaSalle then asks, 'What is it about Stanwyck's rage that makes us like her more, while [Joan] Crawford's does not? Perhaps it's that Stanwyck takes the audience into her pain, while Crawford is all bitterness and self-pity' (135–6). Rather than 'self-pity', the misery is caused by, and addressed to, a legitimate concern outside herself. Her conviction is compelled. As the congregants start to leave, she bellows over the noise of their departure, and then, after jerking out of the pulpit area, she follows them down the aisle, moving between the rows, grabbing one pew then another with one hand, while the other is pressed awkwardly to the back of her hip. The hand on hip (or both hands on hips) is a characteristic Stanwyck posture adopted when her characters are standing their ground and asserting themselves, but here it occurs in disfigured form. Her posture means that on each cry, Florence lurches forward, contorted, nearly winded by the strain. In the sequence as a whole, intensity is heightened rapidly and then, although body and voice are stretched, it is justified, channelled and sustained.

The film moves between grand 'theatrical' spaces and small intimate ones, most notably the apartment of her admirer John Carson (David Manners), who is without sight, and Stanwyck's ease of adjustment is the main reason that the contrast feels bold rather

than dislocating. She modulates her address within the confidential environment. These scenes risk sentimentality: there is the opportunity for Florence to be freed from the dishonest tyranny of the tabernacle and her rumbustious, ruthless boss Bob Hornsby (Sam Hardy); there is the presence of a sympathetic blind character; and there is the redemptive blossoming of love. Any scene including a character with a 'disability' is particularly fraught with dangers: of being ignorant or outside the experience and therefore relying on clichés and stereotypes, of negotiating the clichés and stereotypes too carefully, of exploitation, or of blithely transforming into metaphor (about blindness and sight).

Given these difficulties, perhaps ultimately insurmountable, Stanwyck intelligently presents the problem of acknowledgement, of which manner of engagement might be fitting for her character. Throughout the initial visit to John's apartment, she makes Florence respectful, courteous, sympathetic, pitying, friendly, sweet, cheery, intimate and more. (Another facet that Capra has in common with Stanwyck is his willingness to mix and layer tones, most courageously in *It's a Wonderful Life* [1946].) Florence moves between responses, and never quite settles, not simply because of her awareness but because of her growing involvement. A clay bust of her is delivered, a piece of commercial merchandise to promote the Sister Fallon brand. Sitting down, she says that she does not approve of the bust, and is bemused at why a man that she considers to have sensitivity and taste should desire it. He says that he wanted to know what she looked like, and she responds quickly, as Stanwyck's characters tend to do, 'Yes, but how could you …'. She stops, stares up at him, goes silent for a few seconds and says 'oh', as if she were a little ashamed at her thoughtlessness. The realisation that he wishes to feel the bust rather than look at it causes her to adjust in her seat and go silent again. Her face registers the deepening thought as she appreciates his experience and the hint of a sensuous thought as she imagines him touching her face. The shift in the chair suggests that the thought has become unnervingly erotic. She then swiftly erases the mood of arousal (and contemplation) with sprightly civility: 'You used to be an aviator, didn't you?'

As well as moving with agility between different responses, Stanwyck is willing to discover the depth in a single response. At her birthday party, many visits down the line (also condensed in the film), John is trying, with the help of his ventriloquist dummy Al, to tell Florence that he loves her. They announce they have something to say, but John is worried that she will laugh. Her face tightens, she smiles and says, gently and reassuringly – in striking contrast with the squawking noise of the dummy – 'I won't laugh'. A cut away and a return to Florence emphasise her stillness, waiting attentively, her eyes watery. As she waits, there is something far-reaching in her seriousness: her life, his life and their future are concentrated in her face. Stanwyck avoids the clichés because, at her best, she is willing to express what may deeply matter. An instance that could be too

easily pleasing, or mawkish, is presented as grave and momentous, and in terms of its significance rather than its satisfactions. At the same time, there is reticence, so despite some solemnity, there is no portentousness or self-importance (by character or performer). Stanwyck is able to expand the meaningful scope of the drama without overstepping the bounds of the fictional world (or betraying its other inhabitants).

She has variety *and* depth of address and, furthermore, the ability to allow thoughts and feelings to evolve without letting any one harden and dominate. She communicates the flux of the momentary: rather than simply acting out each aspect to us, each aspect appears to be acting upon her. John puts a musical mechanical toy on the low table and Florence falls to her knees to perch before it in keen anticipation. While it plays and she starts to sing along – 'The Farmer in the Dell' – she makes some movements with her left hand: her fingers first tap the table and then rub the surface, both very

lightly. Her fingers are playing along with the toy, her response to the music emerging in a diminished and condensed version of playing an instrument. These movements are (extremely) marginal and easily missed – they occupy a small part of the frame which includes both actors, the table, the large fireplace behind *and* they are partly obscured by the toy – but they nevertheless make all the difference because they undemonstratively portray a character's experience in the fictional world. This shows Stanwyck's commitment to the moment, her body responding accordingly, rather than the Actor's proclamation of the Delicate Gesture. Capra records in his autobiography (although we should note that it is regarded in some quarters as untrustworthy), 'Stanwyck gave her all the *first time she tried* a scene, whether in rehearsal, or in long shots which served only to geographically orient the audience. All subsequent repetitions ... were but pale *copies* of her original performance' (1971: 115). Consequently, he would shoot her scenes with multiple cameras to capture a variety of angles in one take. She is alive to the scene, which is another reason why, despite the pitfalls in the material, it does not come across as irksome or irresponsible.

It is tempting to call her response to the toy 'charming' though it is without the calculated intention to please the viewer. It may intend to please John but it might be more accurate to say that Florence's behaviour derives from an underlying desire to be involved with him and involve him (she encourages him to join in the sing-along). After being locked away like a performing animal by Hornsby for so long, she is rediscovering the ability *to be pleased*. She becomes increasingly absorbed in the toy. Looking is an important part of Stanwyck's acting: many performers have beautiful eyes (for example, Henry Fonda), or use their eyes expressively (most remarkably, perhaps, Bette Davis), but few use them so attentively to observe and survey others and the world. Her concentration is emphasised by the move to a striking close-up of her face, adjacent to the toy, as subtle in its effects as the unemphatic recording of her tapping fingers. This close-up compels the viewer to watch more intently, but not to point out one thing in particular (a reaction, for example, to a preceding instance in the narrative). The film behaves as if it owes Stanwyck a close-up: it needs to reciprocate her unselfish affection with its own intensity of attention. She seems not at all aware of the close-up, or seems not to be engaged in the usual pretence of obliviousness. Capra writes, 'She knew nothing about camera tricks: how to 'cheat' her looks so her face could be seen, how to restrict her body movements in close shots. She just turned it on – and everything else on the stage stopped' (115). Here there is the appearance of an unguarded, stolen moment, almost cinéma-vérité. This effect is exacerbated by her rough-edged, improvisatory tone as she sings in a rudimentary way (suitably in tune with the elementary toy), interrupted by invitations to John and little bursts of laughter. The child's ditty is performed as such, but she adds a mock gravity, pretending, perhaps, to be a stern farmer, her voice going comically

deep and coarse (plunging on the final 'dell'), and her face contorting.

Even though there is no attempt by her to pose or look glamorous for the camera, she is lit in this close-up such that she does. Pockets of bright light, realistically 'justified' by the flickering fire behind, caress the back of her hair, and the upper parts of her lips, cheeks and forehead. This is the style of cinematographer Joseph Walker: he created globules of light in the darkness, dancing like will-o'-the-wisps, often in scenes with water, such as the one that begins *Ladies of Leisure*, reflective surfaces providing depth and distortion, and enhancing bounce, shimmer and glisten. Although he collaborated on twenty films with Capra until 1946, the style is most prevalent in Capra's early 1930s films for Columbia Pictures and achieves its apotheosis in *The Bitter Tea of General Yen* (1933). Walker, a technically brilliant pioneer, developed a specific lens for each different actress he filmed, and Robert Keser writes that he 'employs the pearlescent diffusion and shallow focus of the silent period for his glamorously lit close-ups of Stanwyck, exquisite things in themselves but popping out from the natural soft-edged look used elsewhere' (2005). This particular instance is a telling example of the way that talented personnel combine with each other and with the prevailing conventions and conditions of Hollywood to produce something singular. The effect of the lighting in this close-up, in relation to Stanwyck's behaviour, is complex, and does not merely adorn or embellish. The light eroticises: it caresses and finesses Florence's femininity. It also spiritualises: it represents the spirit of the self, an inner beauty, the light within, rising to the surface, and evokes the iconography of the sacred, an angelic or saintly aura. (This combination, of erotic and spiritual, has been attributed to religious art, for example in depictions of Christ and Mary.) In his rich and dense book on Frank Capra, Raymond Carney thinks that the director is chiefly interested in exploring a character's spiritual condition, or integrity, behind the social roles and surfaces, and the tension between their spirituality and physicality (which in turn is related to other Romantic tussles between style and authenticity, and imagination and reality) (1996 [1986]).

Importantly, however, the dramatic context is neither explicitly spiritual nor erotic (which is not to deny the undercurrent of sexual desire in the scene, so that her attraction to him, diverted through the toy, is expressed by her glow). Furthermore, unlike the performances of, say, Lillian Gish, Greta Garbo, or Marlene Dietrich, which commonly contain ethereal, otherworldly or devotional qualities, and which such lighting would augment, Stanwyck is earthy and secular. One might even say ordinary but one must be careful using the term with a persona and talent as distinguished as Stanwyck's. Dyer names more obviously 'ordinary' stars, for example, the "girl next door' types of June Allyson, Doris Day and Betty Grable' and moreover he states, 'All stars are in one way or another exceptional, just as they are all ordinary' (58). Stanwyck *is* relatively ordinary or down-to-earth when set against the rarefied qualities of Garbo *et al.* or the 'upper class or intellectual associations' of a Katharine Hepburn (58). Yet, perhaps more significant is a sympathy with the ordinary, which transforms it (and her). Here, Florence shows an unaffected commitment to a basic, mechanical toy, and one that is dear to John. She immerses herself, and intensity is created in the midst of a small, gloomy apartment. This is why she is gleaming. Here, and elsewhere in Stanwyck's body of work, her character is rooted in such a way that forbids condescension, and becomes transcendent.

Her interaction achieves a grace, a spiritual lightness. The lighting also helps her to look physically light, illuminating the finest wisps of her hair and dissolving solidity to make her skin translucent. In many pre-Code films, women appear light in weight, wispy figures flitting around in flimsy costumes, and the effect is not usually so sacred. Stanwyck was slim, and remained so over her career. Regardless of the obligations and pressures regarding size and shape for women in Hollywood, or her own needs and desires as an actress and a person, or the occasions within the films that show off her body, Stanwyck rarely advertises a superficial fantasy of feminine appearance. She is too busy exploring the subtlety of interactions. In *The Miracle Woman* the threat to subtlety, as it often is in pre-Code films, is male brutality. Here we have Hornsby and his bulky body, a murderer, who imprisons and molests Florence. He then arranges to kidnap Florence when he sees that her relationship with John threatens the business. Before Hornsby removes her from public sight, he arranges a farewell event in the tabernacle, and one shot shows Florence in the foreground, sitting at her dressing table mirror, crying, while Hornsby and all the crew make a noisy kerfuffle behind her. Gesticulating and yelling, Hornsby, ever the manipulative showman, exclaims to his crew that the entire crowd must be left crying. Meanwhile, *this* woman is weeping a few feet away from him, and in the same shot. Stanwyck improves this

straightforward irony by the manner in which she contrasts her restraint to their vulgarity and obscenity. Although Florence's tears are copious, she is rigidly upright, and discreet. As she seemingly looks through the mirror to the activity behind, her little finger gently applies some gloss and then halts and hangs off the middle of her lower lip. Stanwyck's gesture might have been self-consciously poised. Instead, because Florence is trying to maintain her dignity whilst apprehensive and mortified, it encapsulates a fragile suspension.

The tears and the fragility feel like an upheaval because the Stanwyck persona is far from the stereotype of the weak, defenceless female requiring rescue. Yet it is fitting too, because she was skilled at portraying susceptibility without vulnerability or submission. Admittedly, Stanwyck's two other films with Capra in the early 1930s, *Forbidden* (1932) and *The Bitter Tea of General Yen*, provide extreme tests of this skill. They push her capacities for responsiveness to the limit and both involve abnegation in relation to men. (*Bitter Tea*, more productively than *Forbidden*, places her in a series of compelling engagements, often regarding vision, and almost defeats its Orientalist clichés.) A scene in *Night Nurse* (1931), directed by William Wellman, offers one of the best exemplifications of her capacity to assimilate with no loss of presence. The Stanwyck character, Lora Hart, a trainee nurse, is meeting Maloney, played by Joan Blondell, for the first time, and in only a few minutes wins her trust. This film is mostly a melodrama of persuasion where Lora stands with hands on hips – Stanwyck once again in forthright mood – pleading with the apathetic and the criminal to behave morally and responsibly, and she is by turns passionate, incensed, and contemptuous. However, it is far from merely being a barrage of yells, moralising and didactic, partly because its sensationalism is snappy (its running time, typical for films of this period, is only 72 minutes). As Lane writes, 'We get abused children, a drunken mother, a wounded bootlegger, and a young unfriendly Clark Gable as a chauffeur in black jodhpurs. He looks like an Italian Fascist and he slugs Stanwyck so hard that her chin bleeds'. Furthermore, Stanwyck's character is not a cipher or mouthpiece; her responses come across as contingent and spontaneous, rather than pre-ordained.

Compared to the pleading elsewhere, this early scene with Blondell is relatively muted, with both characters suggestible. There are no particular expectations set up, so it is reasonably open: Lora could behave in a range of ways, and the viewer is not requiring that she win the trust of Maloney. This lack of necessity and the fact that the scene appears as introductory, makes the formation of their friendship pleasantly unconditional. Blondell's Maloney is gum-chewing and bedraggled, receptive and suspicious. LaSalle describes Blondell's persona more generally as '[s]elf-possessed [and] unimpressed' (135). She was a workhorse of Warner Brothers in the pre-Code years, making twenty-seven films between 1931 and 1933, so she *really* had 'been around' (unlike Stanwyck, who often implied that she had been). Lora says that she likes nursing and thinks that Maloney, in her heart, does too. 'Says you', says Maloney, to which Lora replies, 'Yes, says me *in a big way* sister'. Lora's reply, smoothly delivered to take the edge off the confrontation, is self-confident yet comradely, knowing yet acknowledging, an impeccable example of the way Stanwyck's characters accommodate without conforming.

Very quickly they warm to each other, and more … Lora must change into her uniform, and, as she starts to undress, Maloney steps back and relaxes into a watching position, chews her gum as she surveys her, and makes no effort to turn away or wander off. Females undressing to their undergarments is not an unusual occurrence in pre-Code films, which rarely missed an opportunity to titillate, and Maloney's gaze could be overlooked as many eyes will be drawn, like hers, to Stanwyck removing her clothes. When a male intern knocks on the door, Maloney's absorption is emphasised when, wrenched from her voyeurism, she is startled as much as is Lora. His appearance also complicates the sexual address by inscribing the male gaze within the film, and defining it as leering. After seeing him off, they move into symbiosis: Maloney sits down, Lora puts her leg up and Maloney rolls down Lora's stocking. Their intimacy is ambiguous: they are behaving like close female friends, possibly like sisters, but also like lovers. The casting is ideal because the two performers overlap in temperament and attitude, rough and refined versions of each other. Lora's overalls are still wide open at the chest (revealing her slip), creating a sexy insouciance, as if she had thrown on a man's shirt in a bedroom after sex. None of the scene's erotic currents are acknowledged by the participants (or by the film), who seem to be just getting on and talking shop. By the end of this scene, a couple of minutes long, the performers have got us over quite a few hurdles – meeting for the first time, checking each other out, breaking the ice, winning trust, becoming close, interacting physically, even establishing sexual compatibility – and a whole

relationship is negotiated without proclamation or promulgation of
thematic purpose. (It only takes one more scene for them to jump
into Maloney's bed and snuggle up together, frightened after
discovering a skeleton, but *only* as protective friends.) This
unpretentious and efficient achievement is what Farber celebrated in
the films of William Wellman, and it is easy to take such a scene for
granted (2009 [1957]: 486–97). This is because it is brisk (but not
hasty or contrived), compact (but not dense or condensed), and
because Stanwyck achieves integration while still appearing
independent.

2 MULTIPLICITY

STELLA DALLAS (1937)

In the final scene of *Stella Dallas* (1937), Stella, played by Barbara Stanwyck, pushes through a crowd of people with umbrellas on a rainy street. She is trying to see through a large window into the front room of Mrs. Helen Morrison (Barbara O'Neil) where the wedding ceremony of her daughter, Laurel Dallas (Anne Shirley), is taking place. After bringing Laurel up through her childhood years, she relinquished her. (Prior to this wedding, Laurel has been living with her father, Stephen Dallas [John Boles], and his new wife, Mrs. Morrison.) A police officer tries to move Stella on, but she insists on watching. She stands in a large overcoat, and holds on to the bars of the railings. She stares intensely, bites on a piece of material, perhaps a large handkerchief, and enraptured, she cries. The police officer finally moves her on, and she is ready to leave now. She turns and walks away from the house, the lit window receding in size as she departs. She ignores the cars crossing her path, and her stride gathers pace. She has a beaming, joyous smile. She is getting nearer to the camera, and then walks on past it. The film fades to black, and ends. David Thomson writes that 'she strides away ... daring us to know what the film means' (1981: 43).

Some of the early academic essays on the film, such as those by E. Ann Kaplan and Linda Williams, did not detect any interpretive challenge (2000 [1983]; 1984). They saw the ending, unambiguously, as representing Stella's ultimate sacrifice in a film

where the mother sacrifices herself for her daughter's wellbeing. Williams writes that 'this final scene functions to efface Stella even as it glorifies her sacrificial act of motherly love. Self-exiled from the world into which her daughter is marrying, Stella loses both her daughter and her ... self to become an abstract (and absent) ideal of motherly sacrifice' (16). Williams and Kaplan differ, however, about what they think the film achieves as a whole. As Williams writes, 'Kaplan argues ... that the film punishes Stella for her resistances to a properly patriarchal view of motherhood by turning her first into a spectacle for a disapproving upper-class gaze and then finally into a mere spectator, locked outside the action in the final window scene that ends the film.' (16). For Williams, the film is less straightforward: 'although the final moment of the film "resolves" the contradiction of Stella's attempt to be a woman *and* a mother by eradicating both, the 108 minutes leading up to this moment present the heroic attempt to live out the contradiction' (17).

These understandings are inseparable from suppositions about how others view the film. These writers do not only offer their own view, or offer what they take the film's view to be, they speculate about the view of a 'female spectator'. Despite their valuable interpretive insights (which contribute to this chapter), this is disorientating because these viewpoints are not distinguished. Referential ambiguity is exacerbated by references to the 'female spectator', a nebulous entity, sometimes theoretical, sometimes empirical. Nevertheless, the worry seems to be that a 'female spectator' might be too accepting of, and identify with, the sacrificial and the exaltation. Williams thinks, however, that, the ending notwithstanding, the 'female spectator' will achieve a certain distance and recognise the socially constructed roles for women under patriarchy (something Mary Anne Doane [1988] also suggests). Williams's essay is not forthcoming about whether this is also an achievement of the film and its lead performer, Barbara Stanwyck. In contrast, Wendy Lesser acclaims *Stella Dallas* as 'so subtle an exploration of women's roles and women's relationships that it has yet to be surpassed' (1991: 226).

Interestingly, Lesser's claim comes from an essay specifically assessing Stanwyck's accomplishments. Williams and Kaplan mention Stanwyck only once or twice, in passing, and this underestimates her importance. Stanwyck was, so to speak, one of the first 'female spectators' of the film. Like the director, and other creative personnel, she will have been interested in how the film looks to her, and how she appears to others and herself, and not only in the literal sense of viewing rushes. Moreover, in essays that are evidently concerned with the place of the female in society, the proficiency of this particular female – Barbara Stanwyck – deserves consideration. I assume Williams and Kaplan considered it to be, in some sense, a well-achieved portrayal because of their mostly unmediated attention (and unfailing references) to 'Stella', the viability of her situations and her behaviour: she exists. Who brought her to life?

More directly pertinent to their arguments, an appreciation of Stanwyck's enacting of Stella might influence how a spectator (including a 'female spectator') views the film. The performer is not only appearing, transparently, in the fiction (as the character), she is handling matters in order to achieve the fiction (as the performer). The spectator, simultaneously watching character and performer, recognises this. In addition, Stanwyck's performance of the role of Stella is related to Stella's roles within the fiction. Closer attention to this performance permits a deeper sense of the film's scrutiny of female roles because one is more alive to the mechanisms of their construction. Williams writes that 'the female spectator tends to identify with contradiction itself – with contradictions located at the heart of the socially constructed roles of daughter, wife, *and* mother – rather than with the single person of the mother' (17). If this identification is true, Stanwyck's multifaceted performance is at its heart, as she enacts contradiction, and contamination. At the same time, Stella's multiplicity is achieved without the character appearing incoherent or the performance appearing erratic. This chapter explores how Stanwyck and the film layer Stella within a series of entangled situations.

There is a scene, early in the film, where Stanwyck shows how roles are 'constructed' out of each other. Stella enters Stephen's office, long before becoming a mother, with the intention of seducing him. She puts on a performance of gentility not simply to appear to be of a higher class, but to come across as willingly accommodating. She speaks slowly, with a soft voice, low in pitch and with no hint of the harsh edges and raucous, regional accentuations to come: its carefulness promises care and comfort. Its caressing quality is alluring while carnality is suppressed. Her sexual invitations carry the guarantee of nurture. Later, when he is out of the room, she strokes and squeezes his jacket. Like her voice, the manipulations are sensual *and* maternal, as if she were fondling her son's first smart, formal outfit, luxuriating in the boy becoming man. Suitably, given Stella's sartorial interests, gestures of sexual desire are addressed towards clothes – the physical body absent – and are already conflated with the motherly.

The embryonic stages of her sexual relationship are defined in terms of mothering and good housekeeping. Near the end of the scene, after exclaiming alarm at its lack of shine, she vigorously polishes the rim of a drinking glass. Thomson writes that 'Stella wins his shy heart by polishing a glass' and considers it to be 'the film's most sexual gesture' (41). Perhaps Thomson thinks this because it suggests, and offers, her pristine orifices, or perhaps, sarcastically, that a gesture that evokes the wife as homemaker and cleaner is as sexual as it gets. Stanwyck is crafty enough to imply both and not safely separate them. Stella's cleaning of the glass is also an imitation of Stephen, to insinuate their compatibility, because she spied him cleaning it on her arrival. The mirroring is apt because she will be perpetually adopting representations, and struggling against them.

Her pretty, girlish, light dotty dress and wide-brimmed summer hat with ribbon and flowers make her the virginal village girl on the way to church, carrying gifts for religious festivities, or food for the poor. This virgin is not simply for the taking, but for the giving. Moreover, she is not simply holding the box containing lunch but cradling it. Embedded in the dramatic context of the scene, this cradling posture is suggestive, rather than glaringly prescient. It is appropriate to the subliminal operations of her seduction, but also to the insidious power of mothering which infiltrates courtship and foreplay. Your wife will be a woman who knows how to hold a child. Thomson writes scathingly of the 'cramped gentility' of Stephen, and of his 'little-boy-lost effeteness … [a] pencil … so pusillanimous, obsequiously handsome, masturbatory and … mortified in his gestures' (41). Boles – in one of those apposite Hollywood performances which cannot appear impressive – makes Stephen irredeemable, unforgivable and yet acceptable, representative rather than eccentric.

Your wife will *also* be a woman who knows how to *be* a child. Thomson further suggests that Stephen's taste in women is paedophilic with his 'ideal of womanhood' beginning and ending at a young age, and is best represented by (his devotion to) his daughter, Laurel, cloyingly insipid and asexual (42). In this seduction scene, Stella performs besotted, mostly through her eyes, and eyelids, a transfixed girl with a crush. If her performance speaks to her future as a mother, it looks to her past as a girl – and a daughter. The film introduces a third party, an older man, a one-off appearance, Mr. Beamer (Harlan Briggs, uncredited), so that it may air the unconscious currents in the scene. He comes out with all the usual clichés addressed to a young woman, appropriating Stella as 'Martin's girl?' who is 'all grown up' 'and so pretty'. Despite being 'grown up' she is thankfully still a 'girl' – and therefore not really a 'grown up', but specifically a grown up girl – and one belonging to her father. Although lascivious, Briggs wraps everything in an avuncular and amiable demeanour, as well as bit-part character joviality, so that his comments are couched, as such comments often are, in good-natured banter (and he is only vaguely indicated to be an embarrassment to Stephen). He expresses the vulgar version of Stephen's lacklustre and socially agreeable desires. Beamer's innuendo, 'I wish I had somebody thinking so much of me – hey Dallas?', perfectly insinuates how the young girl 'cares' for the older man (the substitute father), and how easily daughters become partners become mothers.

The film is robust enough to see the overlapping of roles through the prism of incest, while the performers pretend otherwise. Mr. Beamer joyously merges sexual and familial relationships: 'Good to your brother' and 'Good to your father too I'll bet'. Stanley Cavell mentions Stella's 'noisy, nervous brother, the filthiness of whose hands is ambiguous as being caused by his work in the mill, or by his maleness, or by his incestuousness' (1996: 218). Stella's tussles with her brother are meant to pass as sibling play fighting and to ask the question: 'What is sibling play fighting'? Subtly acknowledging the film's own skills with implication, Cavell refers to this as the film providing 'abbreviated perceptual clues of confusion and emotional violence' (218). Later the film uses Ed Munn (Alan Hale) as the 'uncle', 'your Uncle Ed', to push the incestuous and paedophilic implications even further while not relinquishing the sense that it is *merely* depicting harmless, playful interactions. Laurel is only a couple of years old when, ostensibly referring to her sitting in Ed's lap, she is instructed by Stella to '*come on to* your Uncle Ed' (a prescient foreshadowing of a more contemporary colloquialism). Incest is still something of a taboo subject, so it is striking to find it present in a popular Hollywood film, in a mere so-called 'woman's weepy' no less, and not trumpeted as an 'issue' but naturalised within the dramatic context – domesticated – and therefore faithful to its occurrence in life. Throughout, the film relentlessly shows the way that children are taught at a young age to perform, particularly young girls who should get accustomed to 'smil[ing] for Uncle Ed' while sitting in his lap. Baby Laurel does not like it; she screams and shouts. In a later scene, a now teenage Laurel is once again distressed when Ed, becoming ever more drunken and slovenly, barges in and sees her in her undergarments (she has been trying on a dress). He chases her and grabs at her, exclaiming, 'what have you got to hide from your Uncle Ed?' How can there be anything wrong when, as Stella shouts in his defence – Stanwyck conveying, chillingly, a tired mother's impatience, irritation, obliviousness and brutality – that he has known her since she was 'knee high' and seen her with hardly anything on?

When is a child no longer a child? The adult is always a child in Stanwyck's imbricated performance. Watching Laurel get married behind the railings, Stella bites on a handkerchief, and this babyish gesture rhymes with another image of infantile absorption: at the movie with Stephen, where, while staring at the screen, she slowly pushes peanuts into her mouth (although Stanwyck's eyes rarely escape the impression of thoughtful viewing). More than one writer has related her rapt viewing of the wedding in the final scene with this early visit to the cinema. Nevertheless, Stanwyck does not stigmatise Stella as immature, but presents a variety of ways that the child self affects her behaviour. Some writers have also commented on the nature of her clothes in the final scene in that they are, unusually for Stella, relatively plain and unadorned. Yet she is still dressing up: the heavy coat with big fur collar looks like it is from an old clothes chest and is too large for her (intentionally, perhaps, acting as disguise so she can spy incognito). One way of understanding Stella's behaviour at the resort where she dresses extravagantly – and there are a number of ways which I will consider later – is as a delirious, wild child. Before she leaves the hotel suite, we see her putting on the finishing touches: exuberantly spraying herself all over with perfume, adding more and more clanking bangles, and dragging out the long fox fur to go round her neck (like

a string of handkerchiefs pulled from a magician's clenched fist).
Lesser vividly describes her appearance: 'tropical-flowered dress
trimmed with oceans of black lace, a big black hair-bow perched atop
her head (complete with black face net), a white fur stole with the
animal's legs dangling down, vertiginously high heels, heavy makeup,
and about sixteen sparkly bangles on her arms' (234). The hotel
room is a mess, with clothes hanging out of drawers half open, and
others strewn on the floor. A young girl has been let loose in her
parents' dressing room, and is trying everything on for fun, or trying
it on. She might want to go downstairs and perform for all the grown
ups, or scandalise.

The child is one part, alongside others, that Stanwyck plays
within her diverse performance and it allows her, and the film, to
position Stella more convincingly as a daughter to Laurel (who
becomes the mother). Some writers discuss this role-reversal, or
interchange. Williams cites American sociologist Nancy Chodorow,
who in her book, *The Reproduction of Mothering*, 'attempts to account
for the fact that "women, as mothers, produce daughters with
mothering capacities and the desire to mother"' (8). A scene
recognised as relating to this matter is when Laurel chastises her
mother for getting cold cream on Laurel's photo of Mrs. Morrison,
whom she much admires. Laurel grabs the photograph back, and
runs off screaming into the bathroom, whereupon there is a cut to
behind Stella who is suddenly isolated. The onset of quietness after
Laurel's angry screaming – there are no off-screen sounds of Laurel's
activities – is striking and adds to the seclusion. There is a pattern in
the film of Stella left alone, the most important being the occasion
that Cavell draws attention to when Stephen and Laurel desert her at
Christmas and she stands bereft, her back to the camera, in a
mournful, black dress (203). On these occasions, the film asserts
divisions to trouble them. Doane writes that because motherhood,
the fact of it, even the prospect of it, entails an 'otherness within the
self' then 'the concept of motherhood automatically throws into

question ideas concerning the self, boundaries between self and other, identity' (83). At the end of the cold cream scene, when Laurel returns from the bathroom, she remorsefully takes on the 'identity' of mother by applying the peroxide to her mother's hair. The permeability of the frame had already subliminally suggested the unstable 'boundaries between self and other'. Because the camera stayed with Stella, after Laurel's departure, Laurel could slip quietly and discreetly (and apologetically) back into a shot that was hitherto a secure private enclosure. Identity explored through closeness, physical and otherwise, or the lack of it, reaches its apotheosis in the final scene as Stella strides away from window and wedding, leaving her daughter behind. A little before this finale, we have the coming together of Stella and Mrs. Morrison, of which Cavell writes 'that Stella presents herself there, and is received, no more as a mother than as a child … Mrs. Morrison, as the interview is closing, and the two women rise, cannot keep her hands off Stella. I do not say that this clinging is as to a daughter more than as to a mother; it seems rather that the blurring between these positions continues' (216).

This 'clinging' has been enabled by Stella getting ever closer to Mrs. Morrison and the manner in which Stanwyck moves us to this point generates a large amount of sentiment, and justifies it. At first, the butler leaves Stella alone, and as she enters the enormous, expensive lounge that speaks of wealth and of higher class – the film cuts to a long shot that emphasises 'all this space' – she looks around apprehensively. As the scene develops, we will see her overcome the distance, literally and symbolically, between her and Mrs. Morrison, which this room, large and lavish, represents. Mrs. Morrison arrives; she sits on the sofa and Stella sits on a chair nearby. Stella leans forward and, while she speaks, she pulls the chair by its leg closer to the sofa, and rests her hands on a cushion. A little later, she makes her boldest move as she removes this cushion, jumps up and nestles in on the sofa next to Mrs. Morrison. Despite Stella's overriding goal, Stanwyck performs her actions without deliberation so that

they are born of insistency, rather than calculation. Impatient to get
her points across, Stella is trying to overcome the obstructions to her
expression. She is not aiming at greater intimacy, breaking
boundaries or female bonding. Sentiment is generated because
Stanwyck avoids these easy routes to it.

Stella's movements, especially the carefree discarding of the
cushion, disturb decorum without rebellious intent, or defiance.
They are instinctual, therefore more disturbing (and the
performance of the instinctual on film presents a gripping
ontological conundrum). She disposes of the upper-class décor that
so effectively maintains the proper distances between people. With a
flick of her arm, walls are tumbling. Her transformation from
nervous and reserved to pressing and effusive is quick indeed and, as
usual, Stella's effortful formalities do not take long to break down.
Stanwyck conveys Stella's heartfelt eagerness. Kathleen Murphy
writes that 'Stella [is] an unabashed force of nature, messy and

overwhelming in her vitality' (1990: 35), and, according to Dan Callahan, King Vidor, the director, was 'always on the side of vitality' (2012: 94). Her long speech is a remarkably sustained outpouring, and it is effective because what pours out desperately wants to stay in. Stella's effort at persuading Mrs. Morrison is moving not, or not only, because of the selflessness that Mrs. Morrison acknowledges, or because of the sacrifice at stake, or because of increasing empathy, or because of sentimental rhetoric, but because she is also, simultaneously, persuading herself. Moreover, although Stella's articulations seem to form only as she speaks, she is sincerely committed to them, and it is inspiring *and* distressing to see her carried away by her own improvisation. She is frequently halted, however, as she realises the painful reality about to be created with her words. Then *the* sentence bursts out – 'She'll love you just … just like you were her real mother' – hence the bursting of tears (at least by the many students with whom I have watched the film over the years). Remarkably, Stanwyck is performing Stella to the viewer while she is also performing Stella's performance to Mrs. Morrison *and* Stella's performance to Stella. Tears are also provoked by the necessary denial in all these concurrent performances. The sense of a script often disappears in the lucid reality that a film constructs but this is a fine example, enhanced by the dramatic context of a character needing to think on her feet, of a performer appearing to be the inventor of what she says. In the face of Stella's overwhelming speech, Mrs. Morrison nestles into her, and it is uncertain whether she wants to protect this vulnerable child or whether she has become a child, returned to childhood before this wonderful mother (O'Neil conveys an increasingly childlike wonder in her presence). Their coming together creates an instability that cannot be prolonged: the film cuts to a longer shot and Stella pulls away. 'I've got to go', she says.

Although the film has been understood to be one about sacrifice, it is as much about being separate despite being inextricably connected. One can read the sacrifice as an analogy for the pain that a mother must experience when a child leaves the nest. Alternatively, one can read it as a fantasy where a mother imagines the story where she manages, or endeavours to manage, the safe separation of the child (imagining, also, that she is more in control of the story than she actually is). Melodramatic film explores commonplace relationships by conceiving of revealing distortions. Molly Haskell takes a radical view that the film and other maternal melodramas represent an unconscious hostility towards children, and the so-called sacrifice is, in fact, a 'beautifully masked wish fulfillment'. She writes: 'to admit … any reservations about having children or toward the children themselves, is to commit heresy. The only way to express this hostility is through a noble inversion: the act of sacrifice, of giving them up' (1987 [1973]: 170). Haskell's wily interpretation, apart from acting as a corrective and a warning against literalism, taps into the exceptionality of the star's operation within the fiction. Whether they have children in real life or not, or have children in their films, stars as singular as Stanwyck remain, and want to remain, childless. For better or for worse, many of the great female stars are above it: they can never be anything as categorical, or dependent, or earthbound as Mothers. As Cavell implies in his reading of this and the other 'Unknown Woman' films, the female stars are transcendent figures. In *Stella Dallas*, every character and performer is conventional and indistinct besides Stanwyck's Stella. Stars are both inside and outside the fiction: they are essential to creating it, and yet they stand apart from it (because they exist outside it in other films and as celebrities in the media). The fictional character is *also* a performer who is *also* a star, and this contributes to the layering, dimensionality and reflexivity in much Hollywood film drama, and beyond.

Mirror scenes manifest layering, dimensionality and reflexivity in a compressed form. They also tend to announce themselves as meaningful, without quite settling into *a* meaning. Hence the disappointment on reading Kaplan when she condenses a moment, early in the film: 'As Stella narcissistically appraises her own fresh beauty in the kitchen's dismal mirror, she is inspired to take her brother his lunch after all, hoping to meet Stephen Dallas' (470). 'Narcissistically' is not sufficient to represent the modifications Stanwyck enacts, and is misleading. Good performers, whether consciously or not, through the intelligence of their dramatic realisation, interrogate terminology and categories, and static conceptualisation. At first, at least, there is no excessive self-interested admiration or autoerotic gratification gained from her contemplation. Her turn to the mirror is weary. Her gaze is perfunctory and habitual, something to break the drudgery – distracted. Her first moves are a tidying of her appearance, but they only provide more trouble: she grimaces as she fixes the back of her hair, and tries to shove a stubbornly resistant pin into the correct position. Only then, as she neatens her hair at the sides, does her head push back, allowing her chin to protrude. Her face is freed – momentarily unencumbered – and its shape presents itself. She is stopped, so rather than actively seeking self-regard, her handsome features find her. She comes across them. Who is this person gazing at me?

Then she deliberately holds the image still, focuses it: the mirror now frames a photograph, a movie star portrait (projecting a steely, earnest glamour, more Garbo or Crawford than Stanwyck). In only a few seconds, Stanwyck moves through diversion, adjustment, discovery, awareness. She encapsulates, at this early juncture, how practical Stella *runs into* performative Stella. This is close to narcissism, but it is also the exact moment, as her mother off-screen insists that she take the sandwiches down to the mill, of realisation (that such a journey will provide the excuse to meet Stephen). Timed so both apprehensions come together, it is impossible to judge whether the plan prompted this new vision or whether the vision prompted the plan. Self-definition is at one with strategy. She

conceives of her self in terms of something outside of herself. Appearing early in the film, if not in her life, this instant feels formative. From a Lacanian point of view, the mirror enables recognition at the cost of division. As she turns her profile towards the camera, we now see Stella deep in strategic thought *and* a relatively superficial, if gorgeous, image of her in the mirror. The difference is achieved through her eyes being turned towards us while they are accordingly turned away in the reflection where her cheek is also clear of the obstructing arm. The outer and inner are both displayed, and split.

Later, when Laurel departs distressed in the cold cream scene, the film cuts to behind Stella and her reflection in the dressing table mirror. Stella looks regretful, but continues, slowly, to attend to her face, her movements more solemn and contrite. A few seconds later, as she is rubbing the bridge of her nose, she catches herself, looks deeper into her reflection and notices that some of her hair, at the roots, needs more dye. She has quickly shifted her concern back to her appearance, but what is striking is not simply one thing (her expression of remorse) and then another (catching sight of her scalp), but how one thing flows into another, and how one thing begets another. Stanwyck conveys the fluidity of the displacement, and the ease of the transition indicates continuities. Stella's shame about her thoughtless action with the photograph becomes a worry about how *she* appears. This is unsurprising after being confronted by the perfect image of the *untouchable* other woman. The triple mirrored dressing table, surrounding her with images of herself, multiplies the anxiety. For Doane, Stella is not only insufficient in relation to the effortless Mrs. Morrison, but also inevitably lacking against the romanticised ideal of motherhood, 'deficient in relation to this image of unity and perfection' (77).

The nimbleness of Stanwyck's transitions, in both these instances, conveys that when Stella faces herself she too easily starts to prepare herself. It becomes customary: so much time spent alone preparing the self, and conceiving of life in terms of presentation. The mirror enables the separation of the self as she fashions the person in front of her that is not quite her. She creates a substitute or stand-in to go off into the public world, a production, a reproduction, a ghost. Mirrors complicatedly situate characters to create apprehensions and misapprehensions, and indirections. The most noted mirror in the film is at the resort drugstore through which Laurel's new upper-class friends see Stella's supposedly grotesque outfit and behaviour and mock her. It is through the mirror, according to Doane, that 'Laurel finally recognizes an accurate … reflection of her mother's disproportion … It is as though the closeness of the mother/daughter relation necessitated the deflection of the gaze' (77). Another deflection also takes place. The use of the mirror enables a reversal whereby the abuse and humiliation of Stella is deflected through Laurel's embarrassment. Laurel is used, as she so often is by the film, as a vehicle (to divert attention, of characters and viewer, away from her mother, in the way that children do). The mirror also holds Stella at a distance, and painfully reiterates her separation. The haughty youths label her (a 'Christmas Tree') without actually *facing* her (their abuse is cowardly), and what they take to be her is only an image of her. Regardless of whether one considers Stella's behaviour at the resort to be intentional or not, the sequence is concerned, as is the film, with Judgement, and its (mostly merciless) relationship to appearances. The judgement of appearances by viewers, especially the appearance of performers as characters – 'I don't like his hairstyle in this' – is something that narrative films provoke. Lesser writes that the comments of Laurel's friends 'are hurled as if at an unresponsive movie screen' (234).

It is worthwhile attending more closely to the matter of Stella's attire. (Here we need to assess an aspect of the performer's effect that is largely due to the film's design. Having acknowledged this, the way that a performer carries clothes and behaves contributes to the effect.) Cavell writes about Stella's 'massively authenticated knowledge of clothes, that she is an expert at their construction and, if you like, deconstruction' (201). His account was a much-needed corrective to a tendency in the literature to ignore the range of significance of clothing in the film, and particular garments, or else to treat Stella's clothes at best as larger than life, at worst vulgar, or as straightforward markers of class. Williams has said that Stella at the resort 'is as oblivious *as ever* to the shocking effect of her appearance [my italics]' (14–15), and although she may be 'oblivious' at the resort it does not mean that she is routinely so. It is likely, for example, that she has purposefully chosen the clothes that she wears to seduce Stephen in his office. Cavell cites 'the sequence in which we see her hurriedly and surely alter a black dress in which to receive her husband Stephen, who has unexpectedly shown up to take Laurel away' and thus 'her sure knowledge of her own effect is separately authenticated' (202). This is the occasion when Stephen comes to collect Laurel for Christmas at the Morrisons', and Stella hopes to make a good impression, perhaps opening up the possibility of joining them. She removes the ornamental aspects of the dress and this now matches her muted manner. She understands the need to appear sophisticated, but her decorous demeanour does not appear as unduly effortful or as an insincere veneer. Stanwyck ensures that refinement is also part of who Stella is. Elsewhere in the film, sartorial amplification is balanced by elegant make-up and hairstyles, for example at Laurel's birthday 'party': a modest shade of lipstick, sleek eyebrows, and relaxed ringlets, just opening up, dropping free.

Although Stella adores adding ornamentations to her clothes – ruffles making a concertina of the neckline, extended drapes over the shoulder or protruding flowers on the chest – she is, touchingly, self-conscious about them, often fiddling, or fretfully and needlessly re-arranging. Reminiscent of an inexperienced actor at her first dress rehearsal, she never looks completely at ease in her clothes. She wants to be noticed and not noticed. At the same time, Stanwyck's sophistication as a performer and a star inevitably plays a part in carrying off these apparently jarring additions. She legitimises them even though they may be illegitimate in the eyes of characters within the world of the film. Many Hollywood actors have the aura, and the experience, that enables them to display adventurous fashion. A character is imbued with any number of qualities carried by the star performer, and there is a sense of these qualities being present, without them being projected, or obviously acted, or acted upon. The star performer frequently brings disparate, or incongruent, elements to a film. For some, suspicious of Hollywood liberties, these appear as ridiculously inappropriate; for others, their incongruity is adorable, and provides a rush of camp pleasure. Yet these elements may also impart an unexpected dimension to a character, suggest hidden depths, and embarrass condescension.

Stella's clothes test the limits of what is acceptable. They partly represent less class or a lower class. They also express her taste (Cavell's essay on the film is entitled 'Stella's Taste'), and beyond this they also express a style, her personal style. Her clothes complicate her presence in relation to others by disturbing the boundaries of her body. They challenge the conventional gaze (and wisdom), and in this they evoke outré, haute couture. They subvert, even if that is not the intention. Charles Affron writes that the film 'finally demonstrates how feeling transcends appearance through images critical of conventional standards of appearance. The visual energy of [King] Vidor's films is often expressed through signs of excess that challenge 'normal' modes of behaviour … In Vidor's work conventional patterns and conventional ways of perceiving beauty are there for the disrupting' (1982: 72). There is a range of other implications not easily disentangled. Sometimes her clothes may be redressing a lack of acknowledgement (at the resort, perhaps). Sometimes they may be part of a pantomime of lower-class traits to disrupt stuffy conventions or protocol, or a panic at the prospect of them (at the resort, perhaps, or the lawyer's office). Sometimes they may indicate a mistaken understanding of what it is to dress up for upper-class engagements (at the resort, perhaps, or Mrs. Morrison's house). Stella exists between classes, and their manners, and this partly accounts for her discrepancy and unpredictability.

Accounting for Stella's choice of clothes at the resort hotel, where she makes a spectacle of herself in front of all the upper-class guests, is particularly difficult. Indeed, *Stella Dallas* becomes a potent dramatisation of the problem of reading other minds. Film presents characters as human beings often without explicit confirmation of what they may be thinking, and so the medium is suited to presenting this problem. We interpret characters from their external behaviour, appearance and situation. The matter is complicated by the fact that, animated or digital constructions aside, the character's mind actually belongs to a performer who presumably has different matters on their mind. Our assessment of character may also depend on trying to work out the performer's intentions.

Working out the behaviour of character and performer during the scenes at the resort and those adjacent to them is made more difficult because the purpose of these scenes and the continuity and connection between them is not clear (for example, it is not easy to gauge the amount of time that has elapsed between them, or the activity that has been omitted). First, Stella is left alone at Christmas, and she is subdued. Then, the film cuts to the office of a lawyer whom she visits to dispute the divorce proceedings, and she is behaving indignantly. Then, she is in joyous mood during a montage sequence which shows her being cosmetically prepared for her trip to the resort. Then, in the hotel room at the resort, she is shown lying in bed, supposedly sick. Laurel, after enjoying various recreations with her new upper-class friends, returns to the hotel room and requests Stella's presence at the polo match. Stella refuses – sitting up in bed, crossing her arms and disgruntledly hunching her shoulders – but she does say that when she is feeling better, in a few days, she will have dinner with Laurel's boyfriend and his mother. Then, when the film returns to Stella, after more scenes of Laurel involved in biking and courtship, she is merrily loading herself with costume and accessories in preparation for her parade through the resort. Laurel is shocked to see her mother in the drugstore (although Stella does not see her), and both meet back in the hotel room where Stella seems genuinely unaware of the distress and embarrassment that she has caused. The ambiguities created by the continuity might be intended, or they might be unintended: for example, the result of an unhappy post-production. For Thomson, the film does not know what it is doing with Stella at the resort because 'the personalities [who made it] were not quite in charge of the film' (41). For David Turner, however, we are 'deliberately prevented from being able to settle the matter of Stella's intentions at the hotel' and this is not a 'failing of the film' but 'imbues Stella's interiority and psychology with a richness of suggestion and possibility' (2006: 53).

Either way, the variety and complexity of Stanwyck's Stella is aided by the film's mysterious continuity. According to Turner, she gives a performance of enthralling opacity. Given the opacity of film and performance, it is surprising that some of the main commentaries have been so decided. Williams understood Stella's behaviour as 'female masquerade', a concept used by Doane, gone horribly wrong. Susan Hayward explains the concept thus: the male desire leads to an over-investment in, and a fetishisation of, the female form, and the female colludes in order to survive within patriarchal society (for example by exaggerating the female parts of the body), putting on a display of ultra-femininity. For Doane, the female is knowingly putting on a mask, and not all women will accept this positioning as fetish, using the masquerade instead to their own advantage and to possibly subversive effect. In this context, 'the excess of femininity in its parodic and ironic value ends up destabilizing the desired for image, defamiliarizes female iconography and ultimately threatens the male gaze' (Hayward 2006 [1996]: 133–4; Doane 1982). Sadly, in the case of Stella, for

Williams, 'the fetishization … is unsuccessful; the masquerade of femininity is all too obvious' (14).

For Cavell, however, Stella's behaviour is an intentional strategy to scandalise so that Laurel will leave her and live a better life with her father and Mrs. Morrison. Stella's behaviour at the resort may have strategic elements, but in an effort to contest the reductions of former interpretations, Cavell's understanding might be similarly too determined. His conception of the 'unknown woman' in melodramas which feature this character type (*Gaslight* [1944], *Letter from an Unknown Woman* [1948], *Now, Voyager* [1942], and *Stella Dallas*) is that, unlike the woman who appears in the Remarriage Comedies, there is no man who can satisfy her desire or be a suitable match for her creative temperament and energies. Therefore, although these women may be inspirational to us they are condemned to separateness, and to theatricality (and to irony). They have a 'knowing unknownness' (128). Yet, Stella might not be always 'knowing'. By attributing to her 'sure knowledge' and to us certainty concerning her motivations, Cavell may have inadvertently reduced the 'unknownness' of Stella (although his idea of the 'unknown woman' is that she is more accessible to us than to the other characters in the fiction). He may also have inadvertently reduced the bravery of Stanwyck's performance: one which is willing to risk Stella not being in control and one which therefore presents a character more susceptible to misjudgement (by other characters, by viewers, by critics). For Cavell, Stella's plan begins when Stephen leaves her alone at Christmas, in that relatively unadorned black dress, facing the door, and the image of Stella in thought indicates this. It is surprising that Cavell comes to the conclusion he does given that he writes, 'The shot is held somewhat longer than one might expect, calling attention to itself … As elsewhere, a figure on film turned away from us tends to signal a state of self-absorption, of self-assessment, a sense of thoughts under collection in privacy' (203). It is because she is turned away from us and that her thoughts are 'in privacy' that we are unable to assess what she is thinking. She is motionless apart from a very slight drop of the head that condenses so much cruelty and hurt. Beyond that, very little is confirmed.

Other explanations are possible. Turner suggests that her behaviour at the resort could be explained as an 'over-exuberant' act of 'aesthetic rebellion' with unintended consequences. After years of suppression, she bursts: 'she wants to wear all her new clothes, so she does – at once' (52–3). The speedy montage sequence, showing her gleefully being made up, her hair fixed, and her nails painted, for the holiday, could indicate the preparation of a strategic performance – and it resembles off-screen promotional footage of a film star (Stanwyck) preparing – or it may simply express the excitement that cannot contain itself. The montage condenses activities, one thing hurriedly following another, a drunken flurry. When she later walks through the grounds of the resort, with an uncharacteristically affected attitude and manner, Stella may be trying to alienate Laurel or she may simply be exhibiting, perhaps unintentionally, an intoxicated disregard for the snobbish culture. Some commentaries think the film finds Laurel and the upper-class environment to be genuinely appealing (e.g. Kaplan's) and the film does not explicitly disabuse this view. However, the scenes without Stella at the resort appear to be slyly presented as a hyper-conventional, symbolic fantasy, with, for example, perfect, privileged, pretty teenagers cycling joyously down a country lane. Laurel, even by her standards, behaves artificially in these scenes, a doll with a huge, grimacing smile, and awkward shifts of the head. Her earnest love scene with Richard (Tim Holt), where she adopts coy, precious poses, is all pastiche pastoral and wooden, amateur dramatics. It is this ersatz world that Stella disturbs, and there are rousing satisfactions to be had from Stanwyck's spirited display of insurgency.

Stanwyck *also* maintains the possibility, without confirming it, that Stella is disturbed too. She may be suffering some sort of breakdown – this might explain the mysterious illness that leaves her bedridden – triggered by the injury caused by being left alone at Christmas (Callahan is the only writer I know to suggest, albeit in passing, this possibility [96]). Or rather, she has become depressed because of it; hence the mood swings from scene to scene. Although he overdetermines it, Cavell is right to recognise this juncture as pivotal, but it might be a breaking point, not simply a turning point. The scene that immediately follows her being left alone shows her visit to the lawyer's office. Wearing a thick marbled fur coat, she speaks to the lawyer with exaggerated accent and gesticulations, and she waddles out of the room with arms aloft. She may be playing on her 'common' background to disarm, threaten or avenge, with the lawyer as a surrogate for Stephen. If there is a strategy, it appears to be one of keeping Laurel, but the general impression is of unfocused defiance. Stella may not know what she wants and this may account for our confusions over her motivations. It is difficult to know in the sequence whether she is acting for herself or for her daughter, and this expresses the split that she is experiencing. In her hotel room, there is a sense of excess, signifying, perhaps, female indulgence (after losing a man), and deterioration. She lies in bed, her hair tightly curled, all wrapped up in a bow, in the style of a young Shirley Temple, with chocolate boxes and romance magazines strewn over the dishevelled bedding. When Laurel comes in, they chat and, after Stella suggests the dinner arrangement she pulls her onto the bed and close to her chest. A closer shot shows Stella looking out, past Laurel, her eyes moving thoughtfully while she lifts her hair to her nose (she might be smelling the outside world, specifically Laurel's new life, and her new boyfriend). Behind Laurel's back, she can seemingly drop the gaudy performance, and it is this sort of expression, shown only to us, that might support Cavell's interpretation (although he does not mention this look). Yet, it is also unverifiable, and may be motivated by any number of motherly thoughts as she caresses the hair of her now grown up baby.

This shot also brings into proximity the similar bows that mother and daughter wear. If the mother's identity is bound up with the child, who is she when she can no longer mother? Even Lesser's refreshingly disobliging account of the film tends to be accepting of Stella's 'laughable vulgarity' (which I would say the film redeems) and our superiority (which I would say the film provokes and then criticises) and does not consider the possibility of a graver interpretation. It could be argued that, throughout the post-Christmas sequence, Stella is torn between aggressive self-assertion and negation, hence the distortions (of clothes, of behaviour, of motivations). Even self-harm is evoked. The mother's traumatic separation from the child puts intolerable pressure on the sense of self. In the scene with the lawyer, she exhibits obsessive ego – 'I'm' going to do this, 'I'm' going to do that – and declamatory flamboyance. At the resort, overcompensating and overinvesting, she tries to exist again through exhibition *and* tries to disturb the ruthless social order *and* tries to position herself inchoately in relation to her daughter's wellbeing. Stanwyck keeps all these aspects in circulation so that, without reductively having to channel her portrayal into one of Psychological Collapse, she gives a blistering performance of a mother's fissured identity coming to crisis.

Stanwyck's performance – conveying nebulous strategising, euphoric rebellion and poignant confusion, even degeneration – is extraordinarily layered throughout the latter part of the film. Operating within a film that would not or could not clarify, Stanwyck does not create a puzzle where we must ascertain the one correct solution, but keeps alive various motivating forces. Incorporating a variety of options made possible by her responsiveness to the narrative and dramatic situation, she encourages complex explanation and more profound understanding. When, returning on the train from the resort, Stella overhears the girls gossiping about the outrage of Laurel's mother, she sits up in bed, and her face shows some sort of realisation. Yet neither realising that her plan has

backfired (if one takes the Cavellian line) nor realising the consequences of her scandalous behaviour quite accounts for the depth that Stanwyck conveys in the expression. She makes it appear as if Stella is experiencing a more fundamental realisation; and that she is becoming conscious, or regaining consciousness. Her hair has broken free from the tighter perm she wore at the resort – something is releasing. The camera moves slowly towards her – something is coming back to her. If the door closing on her at Christmas is a breaking, this could be a rejoining. Following this, she visits Mrs. Morrison …

The final scene of the film marks the end of chasing after phantom desires. As Stella stands in the rain, the warm, cosy world of the wedding is perfectly framed, and brightly lit, pictured as a luscious fantasy. The handkerchief, on which she bites, is the popcorn substitute and the oral fixation, her identification with Laurel, at least for the time being, still figured as an infantile state.

Yet the frame through which Stella watches the wedding ceremony is not a surrogate mirror, reflecting back her own desires, or more accurately, she no longer identifies herself in the scene, or wants to have a *part* in it. Laurel has fulfilled this desire on her behalf (and the scene, indeed the film as a whole, is haunted by the ambivalence regarding offspring as substitution or surrogate). This is partly why the mother's investment in her daughter's new world is intense, despite the film having repeatedly shown this world to be conventional and lacklustre, one which has rejected her, and from which she will now take her leave. After desiring to be noticed, she now wants to hide, hence the sense of her erasure that some writers have felt. Yet in her relatively masculine clothes, she is free of the burdens of femininity, free from the burdens of her gender, free from all the frippery and frills, and from drudgery's damage to them. These clothes are temporary, thrown on before Stella finds the costume in which she will be comfortable. As she turns and moves away from the railings, the Morrisons remain in their cage but let us not forget the sadness: in order to be herself, or find herself, Stella must leave her daughter, who is also her closest friend, behind. Stanwyck expresses it all (and all of it, or any part of it, may make us cry): the identification, the exclusion, the separation, the transition, the liberation – and the contradiction.

Then – the release, resurgence and renewal she conveys from simply a walk. She crosses the road, disregarding the cars that just miss her as they race across her path, and that further emphasise her insistent direction and momentum and perfect timing. Her pace increases, her stride confident and strong, without the ostentatious, exhibitionist sway. The handkerchief is cleared from her face: no longer pulled taut in her teeth, it hangs loosely by her side, relaxed after all the anxieties. For the first time, her face has an unencumbered joy. She is free from masks and masquerades, from putting on a show, either for others or for herself: a skin is shed. Pursuing her own line, she walks past the camera, out of our sight –

beyond us. Moving away and clearing away. Cavell talks about transformation and self-realisation and metamorphosis and perfectionism (trying to become the one you are). In fact, he goes further:

Her walk ... is allegorized as the presenting or creating of a star, or as the interpretation of stardom ... This star, call her Barbara Stanwyck, is without obvious beauty or glamour, first parodying them by excessive ornamentation, then taking over the screen stripped of ornament, in a nondescript hat and cloth overcoat. But she has a future. Not just because now we know – we soon knew – that this woman is the star of *The Lady Eve* and *Double Indemnity* and *Ball of Fire*, all women, it happens, on the wrong side of the law; but because she is presented *here* as a star ... which entails the promise of return, of unpredictable reincarnation. (219)

It does look as if, in these final strides, a delighted Barbara Stanwyck is revealing herself. William Rothman, similarly concerned with the ending's transfiguring energies and epiphanies, refers to an 'unveiling' (2004 [1988]: 94). If Stanwyck can now transform – into a new character, for a new film – so can Stella. Stanwyck is relieving herself of Stella, releasing her perhaps, at the same time as Stella is relieving herself of 'Stella'. Character, performer and star, in tandem, propel each other toward new variations.

3 TONAL FINESSE

BALL OF FIRE (1941)
THE LADY EVE (1941)

Barbara Stanwyck's two finest comedy performances are in *Ball of Fire* (1941) and *The Lady Eve* (1941). In both, she deceives or cons gullible men (Gary Cooper, Henry Fonda), and falls in love with them. Despite the adulation of director Howard Hawks's work, and the critical treatments of it, *Ball of Fire* has received relatively little attention, overshadowed by Hawks's other justly celebrated comedy of the period, *Bringing up Baby* (1938), to which it bears some resemblance (vigorous, flexible woman enlivens leaden, stiff professor). Robin Wood's short account of it in his book on the director is strangely constricted – not unlike the eight academics writing the encyclopaedia that the film pokes fun at – and hardly recognises it as a comedy. The account, built around Hawks's 'unusual gentleness' towards the professors, one of the director's much loved 'groups', is jejune and sentimental – or more generously, it chooses to emphasise and elevate the sentimental strands in the film – and ignores the film's playfully, and affectedly, roguish and mischievous tone (2006 [1968]: 96). He barely mentions Stanwyck, a strange omission because her presence within the group, and her interplay with Gary Cooper, produce the film's *jouissance*. James Harvey's extensive and intimate treatment of romantic comedy deals with Stanwyck and Hawks separately but does not mention the film (1998 [1987]). It is possible that, like Gerald Mast, author of an accomplished critical assessment of Hawks's films, he did not care much for it, and quietly avoided it. Mast outlines some of his reasons for sidelining the film. Interestingly, although he does not mention Wood's account, he takes the contrary view that, far from Hawks exhibiting 'unusual gentleness', these bookish characters and their world are 'rendered … so unsympathetically' (1982: 357). As a consequence, the film is crude and imprecise, and for Mast, 'the fingerprints of [Samuel] Goldwyn's smeary hand have been smudged all over [it] – in its oversized, cavernously huge library where the professors are supposed to work …; in its rhythm, which feels two or three beats slower than the usual Hawks pace' (356).

A couple of other elements further support Mast's argument. Firstly, lurking in 'oversized' and 'cavernously', there is the photography of Gregg Toland, whose predilection for staging in depth looks to be at odds with Hawks's preference for a lighter, ingenuous, less mannered composition. The layering of planes impedes fluency, what Manny Farber calls Hawks's 'mellifluous motion' (2009 [1969]: 655). Andrew Britton also notes the clash: 'Brittle artificiality is … the term … for the deep-focus compositions in *Ball of Fire* (1941), which could hardly be more inert and academic … Howard Hawks, as we might expect, is not interested in deep focus … the shots … are patently un-Hawksian' (2009 [1989]: 429). Secondly, also weighing heavily, are attitudes and strategies from the script/screenplay by Billy Wilder and Charles Brackett. There is a clever-clever, emotionally detached tone, and a cartoonish reduction with characters and situations thickly outlined. Dan Callahan tersely summarises: '[It is] a movie … working at cross purposes between Wilder's Berlin sarcasm, Toland's pictorial solemnity, Cooper's mannered cuteness, and Hawks's cool indifference' (2012: 139).

Especially noteworthy is the Wilder/Brackett dialogue, which contradicts the Hawks style as Mast describes it elsewhere in his book: 'restrained, natural, underplayed, understated … it is the spareness of Hawks's dialogue that gives his world its aroma, flavor, and texture' (48). Prof. Bertram Potts, played by Gary Cooper, first visits Stanwyck's character, Sugarpuss O'Shea, in her dressing room. This follows her nightclub rendition, with the Gene Krupa orchestra no less, of the song 'Drum Boogie', including a spooky, whispery, miniature version, where a huddle of hushed voices is kept in time by matchsticks snaring on the sandy, striking surface of a matchbox. Potts has come to investigate her use of slang but she mistakenly thinks he is the DA on her case, after being warned by a couple of hoodlums (one of whom is Duke Pastrami, played by Dan Duryea) that the heat is on because of her association with a gangster (Joe Lilac, played by Dana Andrews). She snorts a series of tough-talking, slangy outbursts: 'Cut the corners, what is it?'; 'Get this – I don't know from nothing'; 'Suppose you tell the DA to take a nice running jump for himself'; 'Are you a bull or aren't you?'; and 'shove in your clutch'. Captivating and intriguing though these lines are in themselves, the problem is that they are *so* highlighted, so deliberately *there* to deliver, rather *too* entertaining in themselves; there is this line, then this line, one after another, a list of discrete phrases to be recited by the performer. Such dialogue is ideal for a one-dimensional hoodlum like Pastrami who is a mouthpiece for the boss, and where such speech is part of a threatening and alienating patter, but Stanwyck and her character look awkward acting as mouthpieces for the scriptwriters. The lines come from outside her, and too conspicuously from outside the film.

On the other hand, given that Sugarpuss fears that Prof. Potts is the DA, it may be appropriate that her lines are stiff and unyielding. They are a front, to hold off invasive men, and render her invulnerable. Learnt on the street, they are rehearsed and ready to be deployed. Moreover, if it all sounds a little too much like the Dictionary of Slang Phraseology being declaimed, then that is how the professor might hear it, each word or phrase a definitive *example*. The dialogue may be too constructed and Stanwyck's delivery too much a demonstration, but this creates an amusing pedagogical air to the proceedings. It reveals the range of vocabulary and the possibilities for a grammar of slang: compelling his departure, Sugarpuss tells him to 'scrow, scram, scraw', and although he does as he is told, he departs in delight at her 'complete conjugation'. Furthermore, although the comedy of cross-purposes is contrived, like a sketch or routine performed by a double act, and (comes across as) too premeditated, it contains lines that are smartly dovetailed. Sugarpuss says, referring to her knowledge of a crime, 'Get this – I don't know from nothing', to which Prof. Potts replies, referring to her knowledge of slang, 'but you do – every word you say proves as much'.

The rigidities of the film could therefore provide opportunities for Stanwyck. For Molly Haskell, far from being an uncomfortable mix of artistic temperaments, '*Ball of Fire* is a perfect fusion of Hawks' dialectics and those of [the scriptwriters] … When Barbara Stanwyck as a fast-talking gangster's moll invades the sanctuary of a group of lexicographers … it is as if Hawks had recognised the sclerotic danger of male camaraderie – and was resisting it' (1987 [1973]: 210). It is clear that Sugarpuss's 'vitality stimulates the professors' capacity for spontaneous enjoyment' (Wood: 97), but equally the 'vitality' of Stanwyck's performance stimulates the more stolid, slow-witted, and hollow aspects of the film's narrative shape, style and construction (highlighted by Mast). The film is set up for Stanwyck to finesse, and this contributes to the reflexive and meta-filmic aspects of the comedy. In one scene, the professors, inspired by Sugarpuss, are trying to work out the moves of a dance, by way of compound fractions and complex mathematical chalk markings on the floor. The film uses extreme deep focus shots with one professor's face in the foreground (he is standing legs wide apart, strained and rigid) and the remaining group much further back. The Toland version of this compositional style is normally associated with fraught melodramas (those of William Wyler or Orson Welles) so it feels incongruous to see it used in a comedy, or for comic effect.

Nevertheless, the forced composition matches the professors' straining, and perhaps mocks it, and the style itself, recognising its contrivances, may be undergoing a touch of self-parody. When Sugarpuss enters the group to teach them by example, the new shot is more relaxed, and the extreme planes of deep focus composition disappear. She breaks down the artificiality of the professors *and* the composition. Is she Hawks's secret agent, smuggling in his preferred compositional style?

If the film is testing Stanwyck's powers of resuscitation – a Hawksian task, perhaps – the sense of it being *brought to life* is enhanced by the evocation of antecedents. On the run from the police, Sugarpuss decides to take the professor up on his offer as a ruse so that she may use their 'cavernous' abode as a hideout. As the professors scurry off in awe of this visiting creature, and later creep round doors and staircases to peek at her fascinations, we realise that we are watching an adaptation, or reworking, of *Snow White and the Seven Dwarfs*. (However, they are not all small, there are eight of them, unless Potts is Prince Charming, and, unlike the Broadway play and Walt Disney versions of the story, their names are not signifiers of their dominant character traits – Professors Potts, Gurkakoff, Jerome, Magenbruch, Robinson, Quintana, Oddly and Peagram – played respectively by Gary Cooper, Oskar Homolka, Henry Travers, S.Z. Sakall, Tully Marshall, Leonid Kinskey, Richard Haydn and Aubrey Mather.) Sugarpuss escapes the nasty and horrid, real world of gangsters and cops, and takes refuge in their 'sanctuary'. Here, she becomes unusually animated, and colours their dull existence. It should be a treat to have these subsidiary supporting actors, familiar friends, all in one place, although, unfortunately, having them all in one place is self-cancelling, as they too eagerly, and too pleasingly, accentuate the limited traits of their characters. No doubt a-good-idea-at-the-time, they are too self-consciously gathered together, and their character actor qualities are drowned out in all the noise declaring them to be Character Actors. For Wood, they are treated by the film with 'unusual gentleness' but this could equally be seen as indulgence as they are reduced, with the odd exception, to childish men, or inexperienced boys, all nervous and wide-eyed in the presence of a pretty girl. Haskell says that, on occasions, Hawks betrays 'the sensibility of an arrested adolescent' (although, for her, *Ball of Fire* fights against these impulses [209]). It is not easy to tell whether Hawks and Wilder are using the professors' kindly, cartoonish nature to satirise lasciviousness's, avuncular disguise, or hide behind it themselves. There is no denying the sniggering. The name Snow White may have suggested virginal promise, but unlike Sugarpuss does not advertise the sweet taste of the heroine's genitalia. (The polite definition of 'puss', provided by the film, is 'face', as in 'sourpuss'.) Nevertheless, as far as Stanwyck is concerned, there will be more to it, as she turns out to be sweet in other ways. If that sounds a little too much like the 'tart with a heart', for the performer it is an opportunity, once again, to combine opposing character traits such that they seem vibrantly compatible (sweet *and* sour). She also revivifies clichés, not by knowingly playing with them, but by individualising characteristics, and authenticating them. The mere thought of the stereotype feels impertinent.

The film most explicitly admits its fairy-tale heritage in a dazzling revelation. Potts removes Sugarpuss's large fur coat to expose her dress that is sparkling, *really*, *really* sparkling. Accompanied by wispy music, she is an apparition. When he turns around to see her, Cooper, startled, does a little hop back, and seeing the dainty movement by this tall, heavy, rugged man is itself a little startling. This is not simply the standard sexy image of the slim woman suddenly, yet predictably, revealed in seductive garb because the erotic sight is also magical or supernatural. She is a glow-worm (not a bookworm) with twinkling globules seemingly generated by electricity – balls of fire – and, although we have seen her in this dress before, only now does it appear charged. Particularly incongruous against all the dusty tomes, this excessive image may be taken as a bizarre sight gag playing on the disturbing appearance of the pulsating woman, and on the awe of the palpitating adolescent who sees Woman not only as 'other' but as other-worldly.

Sugarpuss is unsettling, not simply because she is an eroticised, beautiful woman, but because she *makes light*. Stanwyck's agility and humour, not attributes given to everything that is beautiful or erotic, play against stolidity, fixity, and convention. The man is limited, slow, and naïve and the woman is nimble, quick-witted and experienced. When Potts initially opens the front door, Sugarpuss's greeting – a casual salute, a wink and a click of her mouth – acknowledges her surprise visit, and is a little too sophisticated and coded for the literal-minded professor. Rather than a well-worn series of moves, throughout her sojourn with the professors, she is flexible and idiosyncratic. The necessity for deception does not inhibit Sugarpuss's behaviour – on the contrary, it gives her freedom to improvise, and this is the same in *The Lady Eve*, as we will see, when Jean reels in Charles Pike (Henry Fonda). In both films, the behaviour of her characters is not straightforwardly or narrowly geared towards securing the overriding goal or objective, conning the men, which the films have initially established (hence, paradoxically, aiding the duplicity). This is further complicated by the fact that during this process, in both films, she is falling in love with her 'mark'. However, for lengthy periods of the exchanges with her leading men, Sugarpuss and Jean do not divulge this, or indicate whether they are even conscious of it, thus charging all their seductions with ambiguity. In Stanwyck's hands, the initial fraudulence is an opportunity to combine different types of deceptive behaviour, criminal and non-criminal, each one a version of another. It is joyously slippery.

As we have seen, many of Stanwyck's performances explore the tension between accommodation and individuality, and each genre provides different circumstances and possibilities for this exploration. After flicking through a huge volume on Greek

philosophy, Sugarpuss moves across the room to find a chair, and stretches out. Silky, shiny and slinky though she is, with her long bare legs outstretched, we are invited to see not simply an object of desire but a body that need not be stiff, that self-confidently makes itself comfortable. The hurried removal of her stockings is brazenly practical. She does not wilfully disturb formalities, earnest attitudes or obstructing objects and furniture (as Katharine Hepburn's Susan does exhilaratingly in *Bringing Up Baby*) but somehow finds her way through, finds a way of making use of things. She makes herself at home.

Sugarpuss uses her sexuality at the same time as she neutralises it, or confuses it (after all, as she says, 'This is the first time that anybody moved in on my brain'). She must effectively draw the men in, but then reduce the effect to something unthreatening and homely. Drawn they are, for while Potts and Sugarpuss talk in the foreground, the deep focus lets us see the little people pop up in the background, at different doorways, increasing imperceptibly, more like the forest animals in Disney's version of the fairy tale than the dwarfs themselves. They approach the pair accompanied, suitably enough, by Mickey Mousing, pizzicato music, and they surround her, and seal her off. We can now watch her perform within the enclosure. One of Hawks's favourite dramatic situations, much celebrated by his commentators, is to set up the group as a laboratory of human behaviour; Farber writes of characters being 'strangely pinned in place by the idea of people being linked together in tight therapeutic groups' (654). Yet here, while the men remain constrained by their limited character actor personas, her behaviour remains open to possibility. Sugarpuss appears to be inspired by the claustrophobia. Her encirclement rhymes with the whispery 'Drum Boogie' sequence with the audience in the nightclub tightly folded in, nearly swallowing her, and yet she held her own, secure, strong, the focus of the group. Now, stockings removed, she beckons, outstretches her leg, and gifts the phallus, but only so that Potts can appreciate how cold her feet are! She tells the professors to look into her mouth, guiding them towards the painted hole, but only so they may see her inflamed throat! (They are sympathetic yet, being academics, are slow to get to the point, so she needs to insist, with the typically Wilderesque, stand-up comic line, that 'It's as red as *The Daily Worker* and just as sore'.) A common Stanwyck strategy, which she shares with some of the other great female performers of the period, is to take simplistic images or outlines of female sexuality provided by the movies and flesh them out with a variety of modulating qualities (charm, intelligence, wit, irony, sensitivity, seriousness, poignancy). In this comic environment, she merges both the sexual and non-sexual aspects of teasing, in order to lead the men on.

These qualities are best exemplified in the sequence with Professor Potts, when he tells Sugarpuss that she should leave the house because she is too distracting, and she must persuade him to

let her stay. The shooting style is straightforward, more characteristically Hawksian, and yet one can see something elaborate being enabled, what Farber refers to, in relation to Hawks's films generally, as 'personality-revealing motion' and the 'geography of gesture' (656). At first, she is sitting in an armchair, fiddling with her new engagement ring from Lilac, and then she gets up and lollops away from him, pulling at her fingers in front of her waist saying, 'There is a lot of words we haven't caught up with'. This looser pace contrasts to her sharp turnaround as she throws out her right arm to point on 'for instance' (after which she parks her fist on her hip). Meanwhile, she rests her left arm on the trolley of huge books. As she translates the phrase, 'get you on the Ameche' – 'get you on the telephone' – she raises this arm, gesticulates in a circle to round off the explanation with a flourish, and ornaments it with a curlicue as her curved finger comes to rest on her cheek. For Haskell, 'Hawks's women have a passion to do, to accomplish, to hold their own ... an instinct for self-preservation translated into the motion of the mind, into verbal wit' (138–9). There is also a range and vibrancy of gesture, moving with the words, accompanying them, and representing the 'motion of the mind'. Despite being absorbed into the flow, Sugarpuss's gestures are distinctive; and despite being part of an act, they are instinctive. They are accentuated, part of her calculated performance of persuasion but, swift and supple, they are neither declamatory nor mannered. They have a restrained bravura.

Over the short period of their exchange, Stanwyck mixes and matches tones. When Potts says, 'Make no mistake, I shall regret the absence of your keen mind …', her face looks mildly concerned and disconcerted, and her eyes move ever so slightly to peruse him circumspectly while he is turned away. Yet, before he has completed the sentence – '… unfortunately, it is inseparable from an extremely disturbing body' – she shifts attitude, whistling mockingly as he says 'body'. A little later, she comes on all broodingly seductive, nestles up close to him, deepens her voice, and fixes her eyes insistently on his face (and Stanwyck's eyes alone are capable of deft variation). This is an actress who was equally comfortable in a range of film genres, and she could call upon any aspect of them to inflect the one she currently inhabited. When he admits that he applied cold water to his neck, her response – 'A little sun on my hair and *you had to water your neck*' – is all at once patronising, pitying, and threatening, as though she were suddenly a sinister character in a thriller. These tonal adjustments ensure that the drama does not settle, nor settle the matter of veracity and motivation.

This irresolution is further stimulated by Sugarpuss's inscrutability. When he says, 'I too have been acutely aware of your presence' she looks up in hope. She may be sensing a new vulnerability *or* she may be genuinely pleased, flattered and stimulated by his desire. The trickery and the growing attraction are simultaneous and cannot be disentangled. They sit comfortably together because dissembling and withholding are common behavioural traits in the early stages of courtship. For these comedies, desires are discovered, and relationships born, in deceit and manipulation. Only a few minutes before, when Sugarpuss met Lilac's heavies briefly outside the house, she was contemptuous of the professors and anxious to depart. So who's she fooling? This film and *The Lady Eve* show the conning scenario to be ideal for dramatising the obscurities of attraction and seduction.

The film provides a twisting variation on the 'playacting for real' that Haskell recognises '[i]n Hawks' best films … men and women thrusting themselves ironically at each other, auditioning for acceptance but finding out in the process who they really are' (211). Stanwyck does most of the ironic 'thrusting'. This is one reason why *Ball of Fire* does not offer the 'dazzling battles of word, innuendo, glance, and gesture – between Grant and Hepburn, Grant and Jean Arthur, Grant and Rosalind Russell, John Barrymore and Carole Lombard, Bogart and Bacall, Wayne and Angie Dickinson, Rock Hudson and Paula Prentiss – [the] Utopian procrastinations to avert the paraphernalia of released love that can only expend itself' that David Thomson celebrates in other films by Hawks (1995 [1975]: 322). The film is one-sided with Cooper acting as the straight man. There is little repartee or jousting to enjoy, instead we watch her play off him. Sugarpuss works Potts, of course, but Stanwyck also *works around* Cooper. The danger for the performer with all the moves is that she will overwork, straining to keep the material lively in the face of a co-star who must necessarily remain restricted. Moreover, the temptation in situations of sexual duplicity, especially, but not only, in comedies, is for film and female performer to exaggerate the seduction, taking it to the edge of licentious grotesquery. She is not trapped in one crude register. Potts remains in the foreground of the shot, dark and heavy, as Sugarpuss moves away from him and up to the window area. It is the beginning of an unhurried, alluring parade, but it is also delicate and cool. She sways gently, without swishing. Her dress is light both in weight and colour and, in contrast to the

showy glow-worm outfit, relatively demure. Toned down, however, she appears more provocative, and not simply because of the potency of sexual restraint, or the connotations of the girl wandering in summer, dreamy, and nonchalant. More specifically, she presents the fantasy of the showgirl whose pornographic image is humanised and, assimilated into the ordinary, is more, and less, available, and therefore ambivalently eroticised.

Stanwyck's sexualising of proceedings sidesteps tonal expectations. When she reaches the window area, she turns on the spot, like a catwalk model, appropriating another genre of females on show – in order to remodel it. What we see, as the film cuts to a closer shot – as if separating the moment, pinpointing it, holding it up – is neither the fashion model's deadpan, empty mask nor a winking, come-hither, but a surprisingly sedate and sober face. Instead of Sugarpuss mocking the image that had so perturbed him – when, during the previous afternoon, according to him, and unseen by us, she happened to stand against the window with the sunlight in her hair – or vulgarising it, she poses so that it can be regarded with gravity (by him, and by her). Sugarpuss's provocation to the professor, and Stanwyck's to the viewer and to the genre, within an arch and dissimulating context, is to stand there and look genuinely serious. It is acute and puncturing.

Having taken the film (and the situation) to a point of stillness and quiet, and eroticised through restraining (or draining) the comedic, her character then becomes excitable. Sugarpuss says, 'I came on account of you … and not on account of you needed some slang … on account of because I wanted to see you again', and he tells 'Miss O'Shea' that the construction 'on account of because' outrages every grammatical law. This only encourages her. 'So what?', she exclaims, wafting her hand to dismiss, 'I came on account of because I couldn't stop thinking about you after you left my dressing room … On account of because I thought you were big, and cute, and pretty'. It is her last throw of the dice, and it is evidently manipulative, but it sounds frank. As she moves through the adjectives, coming up with them now, like a good liar, she is realising the truth. Rather than delivering the line, moreover, as some tongue-twisting verbal manoeuvre, relishing the cleverness it invites, its tangled, ungrammatical construction comes across as straightforward. Her disguises continue to unveil.

Nevertheless, she hopes her prey will be caught up in her unwieldy sentence. If Potts and Pike, Cooper and Fonda, are barely subjects of the films but objects with which she can play – erotic playthings – they are not easy to get at. They are both tall actors, and she is short, so this is a physical as well as a verbal challenge. She sulks when she realises Potts is too tall to kiss (she is eager to show him what it means to be a 'regular yum-yum type'), and goes to fetch a book to stand on. Supposedly, Stanwyck was less than five and a half feet tall and, as Anthony Lane writes, 'she spent a lot of time onscreen looking upward at her leading men' (2007). Her crackling 'agh-agh' (a variation on 'uh-uh'), which registers that one book will not be platform enough, is one of those scraps of behaviour which is inessential, apparently accidental, throwaway, but is essentially part of who a character is. Such scraps are performed too unselfconsciously to look like 'bits of business'. Even if the words or instructions appear in the script, or are given by the director, the performer integrates them, and discovers their spontaneity. They convey involvement by character and performer. However strategic they *actually* are, they are removed from the conventions of 'acting', and not fully formed or regular enough to be traits or characteristics. They are green shoots creeping through the paving which make the character feel like a person living – now. In such moments, we become conscious that, even in a thoroughly constructed Hollywood studio film, as well as watching characters on film we are observing humans *being*. As she fetches a second book so determinedly, one cannot help feeling that this is the only useful role for books this big, the only meaningful way in which these learned tomes will raise you. She gives a little wobble to test stability, and her words wobble too ('Isn't that juuust tooo bad' is her response to the alarming news that they are Prof. Gurkakoff's cross-reference books). Sugarpuss clutches Potts around the neck, and presses two kisses into him, each one representing a 'yum'. The demonstration of 'yum-yum', which is two 'yum's combined, requires a third kiss more forceful and prolonged. He is stiff and petrified, so they fall over …

For *The Lady Eve*, as for *Ball of Fire*, academic formality, and mastery, as represented by men, in particular the characters played by Cooper and Fonda, should give way. In *The Lady Eve*, Jean, a con woman, played by Stanwyck, spends a lot of time causing Charles Pike, the millionaire son of an ale producer, to collapse. One wonders whether disallowing anything to stand for long is one of Preston Sturges's guiding principles. For Farber, himself impatient with material that smacks of the Weighty and so not unsurprisingly the critic most at home with the director, Sturges is 'the ruthless showman deliberately rejecting all notions of esthetic weight and responsibility' who finds 'the consistency of serious art, its demand that everything be resolved in terms of a logic of a single mood, repugnant to his temperament and false to life' and where '[t]he witty economy of his movies is maintained by his gifted exploitation of the non sequitur and the perversely unexpected' (2009 [1954]: 462, 466). The film's structure, dividing into two odd halves, might reflect its contradictory impulses. A sophisticated first half gives way, largely, to a second half of less subtle comedy which relies for much of its length on Charles failing to see that the Lady Eve is Jean whom he met on the boat, and who is, as his companion Mugsy (William Demarest) repeatedly declares, '*pos-i-tively* the same dame'. Mistaken identity is a common convention in theatrical comedy (for example, Shakespearean comedy), but it is disconcerting within the less abstracted world of the film (or even, perhaps, within the medium of film). The treatment is also relentless, as if Sturges were revelling in the preposterousness. The fictional events operate in a mood of incredulity and a state of self-sabotage.

In the first half of the film, however, Sturges's incongruities, and Stanwyck's execution of them, are minute and adroit. After Jean first meets Charles by sticking out her leg for him to trip over, and literally whisks him off his feet, she moves, in a few seconds, from angry to impatient to dismissive to formal to bossy. After her indignation, the haste with which she takes his arm is indecent. Once taken, she looks very pleased with herself – she's got her man – and escorts him off with a jaunty limp. Later that night, he is in a state of woozy ecstasy, and his vision is blurred, apparently caused by her perfume. He falls – of course – off the side of a chair and, seated uncomfortably on the floor, he is left staring upwards after his head drops back. This tall, distinguished figure is hypnotised and paralysed, suffering from erotic catatonia. She takes advantage of his position: she is lying next to him on the chair, her cheek tight against his upper cheek, forehead and eye, hugging his head and stroking his

ear and hair. While twisting him this way and that with her words she taunts him physically: sometimes she turns seductively toward him, her lips hovering around the tip of his nose and his lips, caressing his face with her breath. As Kathleen Murphy describes: 'she runs her fingers through his hair with calculated absentmindedness ... drops a long nail down into and around his ear, and generally strokes him into a near-swoon' (1990: 35). The film and the actors transform the slapstick ingredients into something more peculiar, where the ungainly and the awkward become arousing. Passivity, delirium, humiliation and contortion: the comic and the erotic, sharing their masochisms, are mischievously intertwined.

This mixed-up mood is ideal for Stanwyck to enact, as Stanley Cavell writes, a 'combination of needling and contradiction and seductiveness' (2004: 308). Jean is elaborating on her ideal partner and she delivers almost every line in a different register, fluctuating with a shameless audacity. At first, she is snappy, 'He's a little short guy with lots of money'. *Then*, dreamily romantic as she defends her choice, 'What does it matter if he's rich – it's so he'll look up to me so I'll be *his* ideal'. (Her voice fails to acknowledge the cynicism of the line. The apparent non-sequiturs are not only between lines but also between the line and the accompanying attitude.) *Then*, in response to his 'That's a funny kind of reasoning', she says, 'Mmmm – look who's reasoning', and pops her lips, one of those unclassifiable, idiosyncratic bits of behaviour, like the 'agh-agh' reaction that preceded Sugarpuss's kiss of Professor Potts. *Then*, she becomes alert, 'Oh yes – he won't do card tricks!' remembering to make this crucial point clear. *Then*, she softens and slows things down: 'It's not that I mind *yoouur* doing card tricks, Hopsey – it's just that you [pause] naturally wouldn't want [very slowly now] your ideal to do *caaard* tricks'. *Then*, after he says that this ideal should not be hard to find, she quickens, and raises her pitch, haughty but also dismissively streetwise: 'He isn't. That's why he's my ideal'. *Then*, croaky and satisfied: 'What's the sense of having one if you can't ever find him. Mine is a practical ideal. You can find two or three of them in every barbershop getting the works'. *Then*, in response to his irritated, 'Why don't you marry one of them?', she is sharp, and screechy: 'Why would I marry anybody who looked like that?'. There is nothing to worry about, however, because she soon comes over all dreamy again, 'When I marry someone … . I'll want him to sort of take me by surprise'. This is a fine example of Stanwyck's broad tonal palette, but it also exhibits the fluency with which she enables the abrupt and capricious.

This fluency is at the heart of a celebrated scene in film comedy, where Jean views Charles, and all the female admirers who surround him and approach him, through her compact make-up mirror. Before we see the scene through this mirror, the film edits around the lounge presenting a series of simplistic sight gags with each of the women putting it out there and putting it on. One woman takes a big swig of Pike's ale – 'the one that won it for Yale' – with a scrunched-up,

pig-snorting face. She attempts to hide this disgusted response when she turns to grin inanely at Pike (and the camera), but her fake expression is busted by a loud hiccup. Jean usurps this staccato vulgarity: she manufactures continuity and her mirror provides fluent, longer takes. According to Harvey, we see 'a series of silent images, with Jean supplying the thoughts and words, and directions for action, too, of all the people caught there, as if she were the author of the whole event' (1998: 567). She does indeed overlay a 'series of silent images' with her voice track but she is not 'the author' of the 'whole event', because that implies that she orchestrates everything that happens in front of her. The description does not quite capture her responsiveness to, and mocking of, the inevitable, and the comedy of a running commentary – where she sometimes mimics the patter of a sports announcer – with Jean as the barbed commentator. Not only do the events take place before her, they have taken place before, and before that, *so* many times. How else could she be so knowing?

For Maria DiBattista, Jean is 'the prestidigitator who manipulates and directs the images on the screen' (2001: 309). She is drawing upon Cavell's understanding 'that the woman is some kind of stand-in for the role of director' and 'we are informed that this film knows itself to have been written and directed and photographed and edited' (1981: 66). The self-reflexive aspect is over-determined by the fact that the mirror image is not a reflection at all, but a film image, like a mini-screen where the image is being projected (or, anachronistically, in today's terms, like a film playing on a handheld device, such as a mobile phone). So although it is possible to claim, as Cavell does, that we are 'looking through the viewfinder of a camera' (66), as a director might, the experience is more akin to sharing a private and privileged screening (of a predictable film with a clichéd story and characters). She is less a director than an adept critic and satirist.

Sometimes she does give instructions to Fonda, one of the many forms of address she assumes, but the joke is that she pretends to direct, further ironising, and exposing, the situation's predictability. The situation does not need directing, it needs redirecting, through a comic perspective (hence the mirror, through which she can adjust viewpoint). As well as satirising, her energy brings a dead scene to life. So if Stanwyck's Jean does stand in for Sturges, or is a surrogate for him in some way (and he wrote the film especially for Stanwyck), it is because she turns everything around (through the mirror), upsets and undermines, and invigorates with what Farber calls Sturges's 'outraged energy' (467).

The use of a handheld mirror is inspired. In terms of the con, it captures and frames Charles but it also expresses her wish to possess him or, even better, hold him, or hold onto him. He appears small and it makes a little spectacle of him but, at the same time, he is something to be pictured, pampered, and even adored. He is something to behold. In the extreme close-up, her hand is huge in the shot as it holds the mirror so as the 'real' film images substitute for the reflection, she holds the scene, takes a hold of it. By being able to hold it, and humour it, the scene appears light. DiBattista writes that the 'conventional gesture [of looking into a compact], which normally signals an act of feminine preening and self-absorption, a kind of innocent and socially acceptable narcissism, proves to be the feint that conceals Jean's magical manipulations' (308). A Stanwyck character once again manoeuvres (within) the trappings of female beauty, and through the mirror, with the help of her commentary, she reframes the conventional.

This distinction between directing/authoring and responding/reframing is important because much of the comic effect arises from Jean's commentary moving alertly and swiftly from one observation to the next. She must keep up with the action and we must keep up with her. One knows that the lines are written and learnt, but they test the performer's powers of delivery, and her performance of improvisation. Our knowledge that this is a successful rendering of densely packed dialogue is crucial to the effect but so is our acceptance that it is convincingly made up on the spot (and that this woman is capable of making it up). Like many of the celebrated wordy comedy monologues, the complexity of each line and the brisk pace are composed to tie the tongue but they receive an assured and confident articulation. This impresses, and if well sustained, exhilarates. It is a marvel what the script requires to be squeezed in, and how Stanwyck comfortably finds room for it.

Although this is a monologue, Jean is the immoderately involved narrator and the enthusiastic voice of all the participants. Sometimes she whips-it-up in the third person ('He is returning to his book, he is deeply immersed in it, he sees no-one except ...'), *or* instructs the 'characters' directly ('Look over to your left, bookworm ... a little further ... there!'), *or* speaks, and reacts, for them, after inserting proper nouns, with satirical and surreal motivation ('For Heaven's sake, aren't you Fuzzy Oldhammer I went to manual training school with in Louisville? Oh, you're not?'), *or* feigns surprise, with pulpy locutions, at their classic moves à la Tex Avery ('Holy Smoke! – the dropped kerchief!'). Pronouns abound and shift subject from clause to clause: one moment the 'me' is Pike ('Now who else is after *me*?'), the next it refers to the emoting commentator ('The suspense is killing *me*'). One hardly notices the different modes of address partly because she delivers it all in a state of sarcastic hyperbole and faux breathless excitement. At the same time, she is disguising what would be jaw-dropping innuendo in the slangy vocabulary and *racy* patter. When a large middle-aged woman tries it on, Jean is shockingly rude, in both senses, asking rhetorically: 'How would you like *that* hanging on your Christmas tree?' Yet, Jean is the one who comes on all offended ('Go sulk in your cabin, go soak your head and see if I care'), allying herself with the rejected suitors. She is putting it on, of course, but it carries undertones of a woman scorned as if Stanwyck was already building in Jean's later rejection (which genuinely upsets her). She lets the indignation seep out of her apparently self-possessed commentary, giving it an unconsciously revealing and prescient aspect.

Innuendo abounds in the film: there are jokes about going 'up the Amazon' and Charles's 'snake'. Jean is invited into his cabin to see his 'snake', and naturally, at the sight of it, she screams in shock, and runs a mile. Rarely nudge-nudge, wink-wink, in *Carry On* style, the performers do not declare, exalt, or celebrate the dirty joke. The necessary disguising by performers for censorship reasons (to circumvent the Code) was a widespread practice in comedies of the period but the camouflage presents Stanwyck with another creative opportunity to modulate. Even when Jean is pointedly suggestive, for example in her cabin when she leans on the shoe chest and asks, 'See anything you like?' – only ostensibly referring to the shoes Charles is picking out for her – the Mae West come-on is tempered with a relaxed mockery of his misplaced attentions. This is not merely playing it straight, on the contrary. At one moment in the evening, when they are sitting closely together side by side at the card table, he gets all romantic on her ('Do you think they're dancing any place on board?'). Looking away from him she says soberly, 'Don't you think we ought to go to bed?', and the insinuation is proffered as a sensible proposition about getting some rest. Only after finishing the line does she look to be teasing again. She waits a second before turning sharply back towards him and stares into his eyes with a feigned alertness as though pretending to be interested in what he now thinks. Yet, despite this attempt at description, the manner of Jean's behaviour here, even on many viewings, under close scrutiny, is extremely difficult to classify. By beguilingly obscuring the implications, aside from preventing the double meanings from becoming one-note, Stanwyck helps create a world of exquisite deviation and deflection.

The film is at its most sly, and erotically infectious, when it seduces us into taking its double dealing innocently. When Charles kneels at Jean's feet to put on the shoe, DiBattista writes that he suggests 'the somewhat intimate ministrations of a shoe salesman with a leg fetish' *and* the 'romantic, even feudal … knight kneeling in obeisance to his lady' (311). There are *Cinderella* connotations too, as an aristocratic bachelor places a shoe on a working girl whose identity is in doubt. Jean, as con artist and lover, like Sugarpuss, exploits innocence and, unavoidably, discovers it (or rediscovers it) in herself. Harvey refers to 'tough-girl heroines who seem weary of their own toughness: that it's nice to know your way around, all right – but surely nicer in a way *not* to' (573). Charles says, 'You're certainly a funny girl for anybody to meet who's just been up the Amazon for a year' and she retorts 'good thing you weren't up there two years'. She could have treated the line as an obvious wisecrack, sharp, attacking, or sardonic, but although her delivery is wry, it is very dry, subdued, almost sympathetic – *thoughtful*. Later, when Pike very properly covers her thighs by pulling her skirt down, she says a droll 'thank you', somewhat disappointed (that he fails to take advantage of the invitation), but also surprised and grateful (for his gallantry). In the comic worlds of *Ball of Fire* and *The Lady Eve*, Stanwyck does not simply tell gags or make ordinary phrases funny (like 'thank you'), she nuances them to complicate tone and address. It is how she opens up her characters while keeping them oblique.

4 RESTRAINT

DOUBLE INDEMNITY (1944)

Taken at first appearance, Barbara Stanwyck's role in *Double Indemnity*, directed by Billy Wilder in 1944, may seem disappointing, or limited, especially after the density of expression and variety of situation – the expansiveness – allowed by her roles in films such as *Stella Dallas* (1937), *Ball of Fire* (1941) and *The Lady Eve* (1941). As Wendy Lesser writes, 'The Barbara Stanwyck of *Double Indemnity* could not be more different from the open, intimate, endearing, mobile-faced woman of *Stella Dallas*' (1991: 242). Her performance is consistent with a film that, despite its suspenseful plot, maintains a relatively imperturbable demeanour. The sober presentation frustrated some early critics of the film who craved passion and fervour. For James Agee, damning with faint praise, it is 'a neat picture ... strictly expert' and it 'never fully takes hold of its opportunities, such as they are, perhaps because those opportunities are appreciated chiefly as surfaces and atmospheres' (2000 [1944, 1945]: 125, 105). Agee is especially disappointed that Stanwyck is not steamier: 'Wilder ... has neglected to bring to life the sort of freezing rage of excitations which such a woman presumably inspires in such a fixer as Walter Neff [Fred MacMurray]' (105). Manny Farber also thought things didn't get worked up: for him it is a 'neatly machined movie', 'slick', where '[t]he love affair seems too slight to drive the man into murder and to give the picture the great sense of passion and evil it needs ...

Miss Stanwyck's brand of sulky, aloof coldness doesn't seem big enough' (2009 [1944]: 178–9).

These particular criticisms go along with the critiques of other Billy Wilder films which are considered remote, even superior. He was disliked by Andrew Sarris in his *The American Cinema: Directors and Directions 1929–1968* which catalogues directorial achievement, and where he was filed under the section, damningly entitled, 'Less than Meets the Eye' (1985 [1968]: 165). Sarris later recanted (in 1998 in a later book *'You Ain't Heard Nothing Yet'*) but the overriding charge was that 'Wilder was too clever and cynical for his own and everyone else's good', the 'flamboyant glibness of Wilder's characters [was] proof of the director's insincerity' and that he had 'callous, morbid tendencies' (1998: 324–6). It is not clear why cynicism, callousness and morbidity are attitudinally unacceptable for films (leaving aside the necessity of distinguishing between character and directorial point of view). This appears to be a romantic or sentimental prejudice. The more pressing charge is that these traits could blinker, and therefore hamper dramatic and thematic complexity, or that they could be affected, or defensive. As David Thomson argues: 'Although he believes in the worst of people, Wilder lacked the will to make misanthropy credible' (1995 [1975]: 813). Gavin Millar's discussion of Wilder bears on the matter of commitment to the material and he writes that the 'danger that Wilder most often courts springs as much from irreverence as from cynicism. It is an aesthetic problem ... he has difficulty in sustaining the tone in any one genre ... [and a]ccusations of bad taste arise most often when there has been a sudden change in tone' (1980: 1084). Millar may well be correct when he considers *Double Indemnity* to be one of Wilder's 'greatest successes' because it has a 'consistency of tone' which is 'chillingly controlled' (precisely the quality Agee and Farber disliked). In Thomson's terms, *Double Indemnity* has the 'will to make misanthropy credible'; and indeed, Thomson goes on to state that 'it is unusually complete amid Wilder's work ... [and] that may be because of Raymond Chandler's presence and the intrinsic tendency of the thriller form towards pessimism' (813).

Mitchell S. Cohen, examining acting style in film noir, writes about the 'very confined spectrum in which to act – an actor with the nervous intensity of [James] Cagney would have broken its seams … – and its demands are physical solidity and mental malleability' (1974: 27). For Cohen the 'most important figures of the genre are those who … brought to the screen a new, largely beneath-the-surface acting style that combined force and vulnerability' (27). Fred MacMurray is an actor with a heavy, thick-set, American everyman demeanour – Cohen writes that he has a 'very American lack of grace' (27) – who, even in less chilly fictional worlds, more commonly performs, unlike Stanwyck, in a restrained mode. Despite his casing, MacMurray is a deft actor, and, in this film, his handling of testing dialogue, often conceited and contrived, is notably spontaneous and unaffected. In *Double Indemnity* he naturalises and embeds Raymond Chandler and Billy Wilder's lines – dense, euphemistic, wrought, and 'hard-boiled' – which would otherwise appear too conspicuous and impressive, and at the expense of other features. He absorbs the lines into the character's personality and mutes noisy intrusions by the screenwriters. MacMurray plays Walter Neff, an insurance salesman, who, on the brink of dying from a bullet wound, narrates the story into the Dictaphone of his colleague Barton Keyes (played by Edward G. Robinson, who also gives a sublimely lucid performance). His delivery of the voice-over narration is particularly finely grained. It is doubly knowing because it combines his character's mordacious personality with hindsight. Moreover, spoken through the suffering of his injury, it is imbued, but not overburdened, with melancholy, pain, and fatalism.

So what does Barbara Stanwyck manage to do, or suggest, with a character and an environment that is 'chillingly controlled'? The films examined in the earlier chapters enabled exuberance; performing within stricter demarcations provides a different test.

Part of her achievement is to restrain herself, and therefore this chapter concentrates on this recessive quality. Nevertheless, she still gives a manifold performance, albeit in a much more withdrawn register than *Stella Dallas*. Her performance holds within it a variety of aspects.

Walter's story begins when he visits the home of Mr. Dietrichson to encourage him to renew his car insurance, and instead meets his wife, Phyllis Dietrichson, played by Stanwyck. She hates her husband, Walter lusts after her and they hatch a scheme to murder the husband and claim on the insurance (taking advantage moreover of a double indemnity clause). Keyes, the Sherlock Holmes of insurance men, gets more and more suspicious, closes in on them, and in the growing atmosphere of mistrust Walter and Phyllis end up killing each other. The fact that Walter narrates is important because the film is anchored in his telling of the story: the film provides us with *his* story and Phyllis is a character in *his* story. This is not the whole, or only, story but it is prevailing. The importance of Walter's perspective is visually established early on when he first visits the Dietrichson home. We hear Stanwyck from off-screen after the maid has answered the door. Her first appearance, wearing only a towel held around her middle that leaves her shoulders and legs bare, is in the upper hallway at the top of the stairs. The shot is from behind Walter as he looks up to her: the film positions this first appearance in relation to his view while at the same time the shot alerts us to this relationship. Even when the film moves to a closer, more direct shot, it is still from a low angle, suggesting his viewpoint from down below.

Our sight of her is interrupted: she is set back and shown through obscuring banister railings, upon which is draped a large decorative cloth (over to the right). The distance and the impediment represent the desire and enhance the eroticism. Films often play on the anticipation regarding the first appearance of the star performer and this, as she is held away from him (and us) and implicitly naked, is a roguishly titillating variation of the convention.

(The towel is low, and part of it is falling away, promising the exposure of her breasts.) At the same time, something of greater consequence is being established. Phyllis is conceived within his gaze, so beyond the fact that she is a tantalising object of desire, she is inevitably obscured, and there is a distance between them (which is never overcome). For Brian Gallagher, the 'majority of shots of Phyllis which are not signalled as being directly from Walter's visual point-of-view nonetheless present Phyllis as Walter sees her psychologically' (1987: 240–1). The film continues to limit our access to her story or perspective, and Stanwyck's performance does too. We tend to congratulate a performer on the successful expression of *their* character but it is equally an achievement to perform a character as envisioned or imagined by *another* character. Stanwyck's Phyllis is not limited to his vision, but it is one significant aspect. This inevitably reduces the scope for expressive variety and risks her character being assessed unfairly.

Phyllis is set up as an object. Gallagher writes that '[f]or Walter, Phyllis is undoubtedly a valuable object, a desirable and seemingly possessable commodity' (241). This view of Phyllis would also fit James Naremore's understanding of the film as presenting a commercialised modernity that is cheap, insubstantial, and mechanical. The supermarket is the representative location: everything 'packaged and arranged in neat rows' (2008 [1998]: 89). This would also account for Phyllis's appearance as a hard, inanimate artefact – man-made – with edges too well defined. For Naremore, she is 'visibly artificial … her ankle bracelet, her lacquered lipstick, her sunglasses, and above all her chromium hair give her a cheaply manufactured, metallic look' (89). The sculpted blonde wig is most striking with its extravagant curvature, and its bulbous, swollen fringe. Wilder thought the wig to be a dreadful mistake (Paris 2004: 17) but its artificiality helps Stanwyck draw a character that is so much façade and shell and shape.

'Draw' is apposite because Phyllis is strongly outlined or as Molly Haskell writes, 'emblematic' (1987 [1973]: 198) suggesting an empty centre. This may be used as evidence to support the charge that the Wilder style is typically lacking significant density. Thomson writes: 'He *outlines* characters on paper – in dialogue, setting, and situation – rather than in *revealed* behaviour … often in his films, the actual images are incidental to the "facts" of narration and dialogue. It follows that the films are frequently [either] bare or fussy' [my italics] (813). On the other hand, from a psychoanalytic point of view, the film gives us the symbolic figure of the male fantasy (which is not the same as the film subscribing to a male fantasy). Elizabeth Cowie, in a general discussion on the presentation of women in film noir, cites two essays by Sigmund Freud. In the first 'A Special Type of Object-choice Made by Men' (1910), Freud describes that the man will fall in love with a woman who is another man's 'property' and over-value her, thus repeating the desire for the unavailable mother (who is married to the father). Cowie also cites Freud's essay

'On the Universal Tendency to Debasement in the Sphere of Love'
(1912) where it is 'only as a whore that she becomes desirable, but as
such she is not worthy of love – a split most visible in … *Double
Indemnity*' (1993: 124). So put in Freudian terms, Phyllis is not
(primarily) a subject, she is the object of a desire that is 'perverse,
sadistic, obsessive [and] possessive' (130). Indeed, for many of the
most involved interpretations of the film, such as those by Parker
Tyler (1971 [1947]), Claire Johnston (1998 [1978]) and more
recently Hugh S. Manon (2005), *Double Indemnity* is not *another* film
to see through the psychoanalytic lens, nor does it merely contain
psychoanalytic currents as many films from the 'Golden Age' of
Hollywood do (especially from the 1940s onwards). The film is a
peculiarly dedicated representation of a psychoanalytic framework
and so perhaps it, along with Stanwyck's performance, will make
sense if this is recognised. For Gallagher, Phyllis is the female, and
therefore 'the other', the object of desire that represents the lack and
must always be lacking. For Johnston, Walter is trapped within the
rules and regulations of society, the Lacanian symbolic, represented
by the insurance firm and the patriarchal order of Keyes, and so
'[i]n her very *impossibility* she offers a vehicle for Neff to test the law'
[my italics] (1998 [1978]: 93). For Elizabeth Bronfen, she fatefully
represents the death-drive, or Walter's death-drive (2004).
Therefore, we might say, following Bronfen, that like the death drive
– the human being's perverse will to disintegration – Phyllis is
prevailing and yet intangible. Stanwyck must render a character that
is striking, yet a figment. She must be there and not there.

Phyllis and Walter's relationship is born in a staged *scene* – the
balcony and the drape, the declaration and projection of double
meanings ('I'd hate to think of you having a smashed fender or
something while you're not fully covered') – albeit somewhat minimal
and abstract. These fabrications are further filtered through the artifice
of movie-star glamour (and Stanwyck's Phyllis would herself become
iconic and copied). On the balcony, she is holding her sunglasses that

return later in the film when she wears them to look incognito in the supermarket and their black arms, unusually and awkwardly, sit *over* her hair, rather than under it. This conspicuous difference contradictorily declares the disguise as disguise, and as a prop, not unlike the hair that looks like a wig. It is the sort of infelicitous touch much beloved by critics drawn to surrealism (Ray 2008) and by those who recognise female decoration and ornament, for example, make-up, as not simply for the pleasurable gaze of others, but as subversive masquerade (Doane 1982). The film presents performances within performances, and further, the characters remark upon them. They particularly highlight the quality of control. Walter remarks on Phyllis's self-control during the crime: 'She was perfect: No nerves, not a tear, not even a blink of the eyes'. After the crime, when Phyllis has to dissemble in the insurance office in front of Keyes and the head of the company, Phyllis is consummately quiet and calm, even when she becomes indignant, with only the fluttering of her black lace veil undramatically bespeaking lies (and Walter later praises her performance as 'wonderful'). It is one of those delicious scenes, sometimes found in thrillers, where the viewer is aware of a character's deceit and gauges the credibility of their performance *within* the fiction (Klevan 2003). A viewer may also be aware of Stanwyck's performance of Phyllis's performance which teasingly builds in opportunities for its exposure. When Walter hands her a glass of water, she holds his gaze just a little too determinedly but not enough to unmask.

Given all the constructions and obstructions, why is there a strand of the critical literature that paints her as *clearly* demonic? For Foster Hirsch she has a 'face frozen in a perceptual mask of scorn, Stanwyck is *noir's* ultimate Gorgon' and she is the 'embodiment of menace: a woman who dispenses death without any feelings whatsoever ... a grotesque in woman's clothing ... with an icy, poisonous sexuality that is unsurpassed in the *noir* canon' (1981: 152). Hirsch puts the blame on the creators: she is 'a character conceived by men who hate and fear strong women ... What woman in her right mind would create a character like Phyllis, who is the product of the woman-hatred of James M. Cain transcribed through that of Billy Wilder and Raymond Chandler?' (152–4). These are aggressive and sweeping accusations, but Hirsch provides no evidence from the film to support them. For H.F. Rey the matter takes on biblical proportions as 'the devil is shown in the astonishingly erotic shape of Barbara Stanwyck' (quoted in Borde and Chaumeton 2002 [1955]: 146). The merciless judgement of Phyllis has not softened over the years. In a recent account, Phillip Sipiora draws out the film's concern with 'phenomenological masking' and 'complications of identity' but does not find any such 'complications' when it comes to Phyllis. He describes her as 'idiosyncratic, ego-maniacal, depraved' (2011: 104). For Sipiora, she 'may be an exemplar of femme fatales, with no positive qualities to offset her insatiable greed. She is a 'cold-hearted manipulative bitch,' in the words of [writer James] Maxfield' (111). Allegedly, even the actress publically expressed this view of her character. After a press screening Stanwyck said, 'I'm afraid to go home with her. She's such a bitch' (Lane 2007), although it is difficult to ascertain the status and context of such statements, and their relationship to what is actually intended or presented on screen.

For Maxfield, as Sipiora reports without challenge, she 'could very well have the title 'Evil Woman' engraved on her anklet ... the label is apparent in nearly all her behaviour' (109). Once again, no evidence is provided for the accusation of 'evil', but given that it refers to '*all* her behaviour' [my italics] perhaps Sipiora thought it pedantic to cite a specific example. Even critics attentive to a female perspective, such as Janey Place, describe her as 'evil' (1998 [1978]: 57). Peter William Evans understands the film to be a scathing social critique of capitalism and patriarchy, and sensitively draws out the patterns of female oppression, but even he overlooks his sociological and psychological explanations to persist with this fantastic label.

Evans writes of 'Stanwyck's portrayal of ice cool, self-conscious and calculating evil', while a few lines later she is 'the image of unnerving and awesome evil' and a few lines further on she fulfils the 'demands of the stereotyped monstrous castrator' (1994: 169). This is despite Evans observing how both her husband and then Walter treat her, bossing and bullying, with Walter 'becoming' the husband (and the crime requiring that he masquerade as him). What of the critics, equally cruel and unremitting, 'becoming' the husband? The descriptions of Phyllis border on hysteria, and if she is so *evidently* horrendous why does this need to be repeatedly and insistently asserted? Perhaps the integrity of her containment prompts the abuse, a desperate response to being shut out by the woman who appears unmoved.

These reductive assessments make the character and the performance sound far less allusive (and elusive) than they actually are. Stanwyck and the film may give us the outline of the 'femme fatale' – an attractive and seductive woman who will cause distress to the man who becomes involved with her – but this does not mean she completes the stereotype, or is the heinous figure characterised in the commentaries. Julie Grossman in her recent book, *Rethinking the Femme Fatale in Film Noir*, claims that the 'femme fatale', the so-called bad woman, is in fact often shown by the films to be a victim of 'social rules' and 'gender roles'. The 'femme fatale' is characteristically not 'demonized' by the films but by the critics and their 'reading practices' who 'overidentify' with and 'overinvest' in the 'femme fatale' construction (2009: 2). Grossman is also wary of the corrective counter-argument, put by commentators such as Place, who celebrate the tough, powerful, unconventional, transgressive, and glamorous women who are a challenge to patriarchal forces and destabilise the male (a force that outlives their punishment within the films). The against-the-grain argument, as proposed by Place, according to Grossman, suffers from 'role modeling as the foundation for feminist discussion': she writes, 'Such narrow understanding of what is feminist – characters who are recognizably activist, who model behavior that we imagine might empower women in the "real world" – short-circuits attention to the patriarchal social scripts presented in film noir. In other words, a female character may not in herself be feminist, but her story may be' (6). In a similar vein, and cited by Grossman, Andrew Britton writes, 'It is not necessary to formulate "positive images" of female strength, resistance or independence in order to produce a narrative that criticises patriarchy from a woman's point of view, and many works of the greatest dramatic and ideological power have chosen instead to represent the tragic waste or perversion of a woman's struggle for autonomy and self-definition in the context of an implacably hostile and oppressive culture' (Britton 1994: 214). Moreover, in relation to Phyllis, this positive image of strength, like the evil 'femme fatale' tag, is too forceful a conception.

Strangely, however, even for Grossman, Phyllis is the exception that proves the rule. She is 'one of the very few (I would argue) "pure" "femme fatales"' and one of the 'few really bad women' (18, 22). Grossman argues that the 'depiction of "femme fatales" frequently attributes an "inner life" to these women which allows us to read them as sympathetic characters' (23). *Double Indemnity* does not obviously give Phyllis an 'inner life', or give us easy access to it, which makes our assessment of her more difficult. Grossman understands Phyllis as 'opaque' and therefore sees her as one of the 'canonical baddies' (44). Andrew Dickos writes, on the contrary, that 'it is precisely her opaqueness that defines the inadequacy of our attempt to dismiss [Phyllis] as merely a cold-blooded murderer' (2002: 157).

Even though Grossman recognises that, in general, 'noir females are presented in a context that helps us to understand why they behave the way they do' (44), she does not think that Phyllis is provided with one. There is much evidence to the contrary, and it is worth devoting a little time to the film's plot because it is important in establishing the context for Stanwyck's performance of Phyllis. She is a nurse who has entered into a loveless and abusive marriage (she says he gets drunk and hits her). The film does nothing to counter that claim, and its presentation of the husband is unsympathetic. The Dietrichson home, so often referred to as the 'femme fatale' lair, is equally a domestic prison with the husband as boorish gatekeeper. In the pivotal scene in Walter's apartment, she explains her predicament. She sits tightly to one side of the sofa with her legs pulled up, anxious *and* relaxed enough for a psychological confession (and not at all seductive or confidently expansive). Her husband forbids a divorce for financial reasons, and when Walter points out that he once had plenty of money she replies 'Yes he had, and I *wanted* a home'. Her delivery evokes the desire and the ruthlessness, but there is a sense of reflection too, and candour (while the pensive fiddling with her glass also indicates admission). She admits to social climbing and provides an explanation as she paints a picture of (particularly female) dependencies. Nothing in her behaviour resembles the moral abstraction of 'evil'. One can take her explanations to be lies, excuses or the height of cunning. Yet writers on the film have not explained why her behaviour or the film's presentation in such a moment would definitely lead to these conclusions. The generic and narrative context provides another opportunity for Stanwyck to unsettle easy understandings of the sincere, not merely to present the insincere.

Although Phyllis sees Walter as an opportunity to escape her marriage and she inquires first about the possibility of 'accident insurance', *he* formulates the plan and raises the greedy stakes by suggesting they exploit the double indemnity clause. He presses her to go through with it. The instigator becomes the accomplice and this is consistent with the film's presentation of a male fantasy of power and control. Quite a lot of writers, using plot points as evidence, turn what the film carefully presents as only possibilities, red herrings even – bait for those wishing to accuse and demonise

Phyllis – into fact. As soon as the husband is dead, Walter presumes that she ruthlessly begins a sexual relationship with Lola Dietrichson's boyfriend Nino Zachetti (Byron Barr). Later, she insists this is untrue: she has not slept with him and was using Zachetti as insurance when Walter made it clear that *he* didn't want to see her again. Indeed, she spends most of the film dismayed that she has to be apart from Walter. Despite her protestations, he defends their separation as entirely necessary for the cover-up. This is ostensibly reasonable and the plot is constructed so the defence appears credible. Psychoanalytically speaking, however, the plot provides his cover story, keeping him away from the woman he once desired, but now necessarily despises. There is an accusation made by Lola (Jean Heather), Mr. Dietrichson's disgruntled daughter by his first marriage, that Phyllis, her stepmother, killed, or hastened the death, of her mother. This murder is unambiguous in Cain's novel, where Phyllis is a malicious killer who kills the children in her care too (for details of the changes see Richard Schickel [2010 (1992)]). The film positions it as hearsay by not corroborating it, and by signalling that Lola is emotionally involved and not a reliable source. This is one of many examples where Chandler and Wilder have gone out of their way to tell a different story. However much Phyllis is implicated in the murder of her husband, and may have desired it, she does not fit the vicious descriptions.

Stanwyck makes Phyllis difficult to read, so it is surprising that she has been interpreted so transparently. A little after her first appearance in the towel, she comes down the stairs, puts on her lipstick, and says, 'Neff is the name isn't it?' to which he replies, 'Two ffs like in Philadelphia – if you know the story? ... *The Philadelphia Story*'. In the mirror, her eyes rise, and she halts the application of lipstick; she is stopped by his reply, closes the lipstick with a swift click, and does not smile. She appears unimpressed by the contrived patter, disconcerted or contemptuous perhaps, but it is difficult to know exactly because she remains guarded, and quickly moves the moment on: 'Suppose we sit down', she says. (Stanwyck's performance fleetingly suggests the trapped 'housewife' who has kept her opinions to herself, and whose capacity for good judgement is underrated because she is mostly unheard.) Rather than sitting in the centre of a big armchair (her husband's?), she pushes into the corner of it. She looks swamped, vulnerable, further exacerbated by his position, sitting on the sofa arm, looking down at her, his virile sales patter casual but forceful. They adopt similar positions during her confessional in Walter's apartment. Seen through the 'femme fatale' lens she is demonstratively, and manipulatively, seeking sympathy and rescue. She is the little girl all dressed up for daddy, willingly submissive, and yet in control. At the same time, her position evokes a way of life: a little overwhelmed, knocking about in a big house, on her own, out of place, backed into a corner, diminished.

Phyllis's inhibited behaviour contrasts to the hyperbole of the commentaries. Christine Gledhill argues that the noir 'heroine's characterization is itself fractured' and 'though the heroines of film noir, by virtue of male control of the voice-over, flashback structure, are rarely accorded ... full subjectivity and [a] fully expressed point of view ... their *performance* of the roles accorded them in this form of male story-telling foregrounds the fact of their image as an artifice and suggests another place behind the image where the woman might be' (1998 [1978]: 31). Similarly, Lesser, another critic not sucked into the 'femme fatale' tirade with regards to Phyllis, writes that despite the 'stiff blonde helmet, her body rigidly controlled and encased ... something of Stanwyck creeps through the mask, if only a hint ... that there is some other kind of soul ... lying in hiding behind that tough exterior' (242). The bravery of the Stanwyck performance is to 'hint' because the temptation would be either to play a villain for all it is worth or to signal that the character, underneath the mask, is incontrovertibly redeemable and sympathetic (even if she is). Both presentations would make things easier for the viewer. For Lesser, Wilder's film is about inaccessibility, 'constantly leading us to believe that something is going on in Phyllis's mind which we don't have access to' (243) – and this is partly evidenced by Wilder and Chandler's removal of the novel's certainty.

An example of this hinting occurs in a 'set-piece' exchange concerning 'speeding', justifiably celebrated and often quoted, when Walter and Phyllis first meet in the Dietrichson house. Kate Stables smartly describes the 'exchange [as] a consummate example of the male-female verbal tennis of classic noir, with the *femme fatale* putting the spin on the ball. Phyllis, as traffic cop, "regulates" the speed of Neff's approaches, proposes to punish his transgression, and ends their exchange with a reminder of her status and that of her husband/"master"'' (1998 [1978]: 176). Yet, Phyllis's regulations go beyond those one might expect in the sub/dom role-play. When he gets fresh, Phyllis tells him that 'There's a speed limit in this state, Mr Neff, 45 miles an hour', and Stanwyck *also* takes her foot off the gas, her delivery gently solemn, almost hushed. Easily read as playing hard to get, her stare at him is not merely a performance of punishment but a frank rebuke. Handling the exchange with equanimity and just enough reticence, Stanwyck shows that Phyllis has the intelligence to play Walter's game without indulging it (and this is regardless of whether the low-key approach is still a turn-on for him, or the viewer). When he asks 'How fast was I going, officer?', she lowers her eyelids, glancing away from him to give the answer a moment's consideration, and then says 'I'd say around 90'; and her delivery is considerate, agreeable, almost obliging. The pitfall for performers of this type of dialogue is to revel in the lines and be over-delighted at being made to look clever, cool or sexy by the script. MacMurray is not unwilling to court this criticism because this is how he wants Walter to appear, and how Walter wants to appear, but Stanwyck's soft handling of the hard-boiled double entendre, adds another dimension to the exchange. She appropriates the role-play even while adroitly participating in it. As Phyllis's dialogue speaks of pain and punishment – 'Suppose I have to whack you over the knuckles?' – her eyes move from his chest up to his face. She seems to be betraying a more substantial attraction, covertly instigating intimacy.

Nevertheless, there has been a tendency to associate Phyllis, explicitly or implicitly, with an aggressive sexuality. The film does indeed present the iconography of the 'sexy' figure in her 1940s American noir guise: the shapely female outline, cigarettes with trails of smoke, provocative dress and the lack of it, sunglasses, weaponry, and mirrors. However, we should take care when extracting and isolating iconography, conventions and signifiers from their use in a specific dramatic context. Phyllis's anklet is worth discussing in this regard. We initially catch sight of the anklet in the famous close shot of Phyllis's legs, below the knee, when she first walks down the stairs. The opening of the film, as we have seen, has been situated in terms of Walter's perspective. The shot of her legs fragments her body and it would be fetishistic even without the anklet. Yet, Phyllis's movements interrupt 'the gaze' or do not quite go along with it. Her descent, in cumbersome shoes, is heavy-footed, clunky and, as one has to be in high heels, careful (and as the shoes hit the stairs, despite the musical theme also playing, the thudding sound is prominent). Moreover, as Walter rightly points out, there is that 'silly staircase' between them, and the score is earnestly melodious, almost regretful. The shot of her legs is a signifier without the appropriate erotic effect, or in Wilder's terms, via Ernst Lubitsch, a joke undercutting lasciviousness and not an invitation to it. When the camera moves back to take in her whole body, she is in the middle of fastening the buttons of her garments, not suggestively but practically – buttoning up. Walking to the mirror, she says, puffing up her hair, 'I hope I've got my face on *straight*', which matter-of-factly admits the tools of the trade and the performance, and is dutiful rather than enticing. All may be surface and appearance in *Double Indemnity*, but even the surfaces and appearances are held at arm's length, neutralised through unsentimental acknowledgement (by characters and film).

This attitude saps the surfaces so that they are dried out (hence all the dust swirling in the Dietrichson home).

After this scene, Walter lustfully describes the way the anklet cuts into the surface of her flesh. This thought is communicated through his voice-over narration which overlays a shot of her legs once again descending the stairs (on a different occasion). The shot appears to be brought into being by him. At the same time, the shot and her leg are not nearly close, or still, enough for the viewer to concentrate on the anklet. All the pleasure (and pain) is conjured in his mind's eye and is not matched by the film's imagery. This is an example of the way the film and Phyllis are associated with Walter's perspective, but are not beholden to it. Some of the literature, like Walter, also tends to extract the anklet from its situation in the film and over-glamourise it. Although Phyllis has her legs crossed, inevitably raising her foot, she hardly 'waves [it]', as Paula Rabinovitz claims, 'ostentatiously in his face' (2002: 172). The fluffy pompoms on her shoes are more ostentatious and distracting, and the anklet relatively indistinct. More significant is Walter's rapt attention to the anklet *despite* Phyllis's behaviour and the camera's (which refuses to emphasise it). When he mentions it, Stanwyck's handling of the response is exquisitely subdued. Phyllis does not reply and her sober expression makes her response similar to the one she gave to his joke (about *The Filadelfia Story*). As she uncrosses her legs, she holds her knees together and placidly shelters the left foot with the anklet behind the right. She is possibly being coy, but her steady demeanour makes this unlikely. Perhaps she is being prudish. Perhaps she finds his insinuations over-familiar and intrusive. Anyway, she keeps herself to herself.

Just as the anklet may not be sexually goading, so her lipstick may not be an instrument of phallic power. Her fingertips continue to fiddle with the lipstick as she speaks and she repeatedly looks down to it before looking out to him again. She gets up and rotates it as she walks back and forth by the fireplace. These gestures indicate

that she is calculating but also, given the thoughts of murder now circling in her mind, they also suggest thoughtfulness, wariness, and irresolution. Stanwyck does not crystallise. Yet again, she uses a context of deceit in a film not merely for her character to appear devious but to forestall making plain. On Walter's next visit when Phyllis serves him tea, she has clearly been preparing to advance the plan. Disconcertingly, Stanwyck performs her nervous gestures – twisting her ring, stroking the handle of the jug, patting the table, and being artificially punctilious about arranging the cushions – tentatively. One cannot easily tell, therefore, whether they simply indicate that Phyllis is lying, or that she wishes to look more gauche than she actually is, or that she is apprehensive in an inchoate situation.

The anklet could be part of a dress code that consists of various items, decorations and accessories – 'puffy high-heeled mules' (Rabinovitz: 172), clunky bracelet and ring, indiscreet make-up, gregarious folds and pleating, and, of course, the wig – which have sexual associations, even professional sexual associations, but which have been absorbed into an everyday style or uniform, and sedated. In the later scene in his apartment, Walter says, as they kiss, that he is 'crazy' about Phyllis but, instead of complimenting her, he makes an enquiry about the perfume she is wearing: rather than being drawn to her, he is drawn to an aura around her. Walter's attraction to the cheap perfume is another sly indication of what is taking his fancy these days, but *she* cannot recall its name. She does inform him it is from Ensenada. According to Schickel, Ensenada is 'a resort just over the Mexican border, which in those days featured a casino and catered to a fast crowd that was not quite the right crowd in Los Angeles' (2010 [1992]: 44). For Schickel, the anklet, and no doubt the perfume, signifies 'lower middle-class commonness, just the sort of adornment a former nurse who has married upward might favor' (41). Wilder may have intended some mockery, but Stanwyck is able to wear clothes and accessories, as in *Stella Dallas*, that invite condescension (because of their cheapness and tastelessness) but which *she* does not treat condescendingly. Her characters exude an individuality and integrity that is unaffected and self-possessed such that, despite the societal connotations, clichéd or otherwise, they have a sincere investment in their appearance. Thomson points out (discussing Douglas Sirk's films, not Stanwyck) that the medium of film has a special capacity to 'pick out the seriousness in vulgarity without condescension' (702). If so, this is another way in which Stanwyck has an affinity with the medium. She credibly carries gaudy or apparently vulgar elements of costume: they seem part of her, rather than determinedly ostentatious, and this rescues them from camp and parody. Furthermore, because Phyllis refuses to flaunt, the clothes carry a variety of meaningful traces. The wig, for example, is all at once, a signifier of 'lower middle-class commonness'; a cartoon exaggeration of female shapelessness; an iconic homage to LA, movie-star glamour; an item in a theatrical role-play, a dominatrix crown; a defensive, protective helmet against male intrusion; *and* something uniquely, idiosyncratically, belonging to Phyllis. When Walter interrupts their discussion about insurance to return to the matter of the anklet, he asks, 'Wish you'd tell me what's engraved on that anklet', and she replies, unassumingly, 'Just my name'.

Yet who is 'Phyllis Dietrichson'? Bronfen sees the film, in terms outlined by Stanley Cavell, as a tragedy of failed acknowledgement, where Walter makes no attempt to see the real Phyllis, and therefore avoids her. Hence, the many occasions in the film where they are side-by-side: in the car during the murder, and most notably in the supermarket sequences as they shift, crab-like, down the aisles. For Lesser, the film is about the 'indirectness of intimacy' or the difficulty of achieving intimacy, and as well as local patterns of diversion there are larger, structural ones: for example, the story being told via Walter in flashback and his relationship with Keyes substituting for his one with Phyllis (which itself is subject to deflections). Lesser makes the perspicacious point that the film structurally depends on withholding a quality of the Stanwyck persona: 'The relationship between Neff and Keyes is by far the most intimate in the film – as if it benefits by siphoning off the intimacy which Barbara Stanwyck normally creates, but which she is artificially prevented from creating here' (246).

Immediately after their first kiss, and their first significant sexual encounter, Walter orders Phyllis to 'get a couple of glasses', and so begins his obsessive supervising of her. Manon argues that his ordering her around arises because of a persistent avoidance of sex, and that Walter favours a 'horizon of anticipation' and 'ongoing manipulation over goal attainment' in a film whose drama is systematically played out on a 'terrain of lack' (18–22). From this perspective, their 'traffic cop' exchange is erotic perhaps but a substitute for sex, not a prelude to it. This fits with the performers' delivery of the lines: coolly efficient, self-possessed and, in his case at least, onanistic. Despite the innuendo, their exchange does not come across as hot or passionate, in the way that Agee and Farber desired, in the manner, say, of Humphrey Bogart and Lauren Bacall's engagement in *To Have and Have Not* (1944). More than role-play, Harry Morgan and 'Slim' are involved in an intense foreplay with words that is a clear indication of good sex to come. For Tyler, in his famous interpretation, Keyes is Walter's real object of desire, and he draws attention to the film's homosexual subtext. Manon, however, thinks that Keyes is the figure who justifies the avoidance so that Phyllis, the 'beloved', is 'endlessly deferred'. Consequently, she is positioned 'in relation to a *beyond*' (31). This fits with Evans's description of Phyllis as 'beyond sexuality' and 'not the self-consciously sexual dark lady' (169). Even when Phyllis is tempting Walter into a course of action, during his second visit to the Dietrichson home, she is not particularly alluring, and this is encapsulated by her desire to serve him tea, instead of something more intoxicating. He comes on to her with a suggestive joke, but Phyllis diffuses and does not take advantage. In another one of those moments when Stanwyck complicates tone with a fleeting gesture or expression, she brushes him off by saying 'Fresh', almost under her breath, in an unimpressed, and understated, 'I've seen it all before' manner, and plops a slice of the lemon in his glass while moving away. As we saw in *Ball of Fire*, Stanwyck can downplay brazen sexiness in situations where it might be customary. Equally, she is not playing the aloof, and provocatively unattainable, woman. She discovers unusual dimensions in familiar, risqué scenarios, and upsets the characteristic currents of desire.

Phyllis is at her most sexually enticing when she first arrives at his apartment – her 'hello' at the door is low and mellow and provides the surprising crescendo to the high-pitched, strained, thriller music – but this manifests as rigidity trying to present itself as supple, compliant, and available. Murphy writes that '[t]he voice can be silky, with a slight, sexy rasp, but the mouth is always as tight and stiff as a marionette's' (1990: 35). She takes off her coat to reveal the soft, white, fluffy, angora sweater, but constriction has not been surrendered. The sweater is figure-hugging, like a second skin, and has a high neckline that cuts across just below her throat. The straps of her brassiere, visible behind the thin fabric, fasten her. After her coat is removed, she fastidiously straightens her sleeve to remain streamlined, and correctly packaged. Phyllis is insecurely poised between inviting tenderness and duress. Walter opts for the latter, grabs her upper arms and squeezes them extremely tightly; their kiss is equally hard and intransigent, and although it does relax, it cannot escape its masochistic and sadistic underpinnings. A little later, in the same scene, while he egotistically declares his commitment to the murder plan, where nothing they do must be 'weak', he is gripping her arms again. She exclaims, with some distress, that he is hurting her.

Perhaps he hopes that by grabbing her he will be able to feel more, but he will never find sexual satisfaction and neither will she. Tyler witheringly states, 'both know that one of them does not get or give satisfaction in sexual relations' (176). The film represents this lack with an ellipsis. They hug on the sofa, and Walter says, 'She started crying softly like the rain on the window'. What happens next between them is not shown. When we return to them, he is lying on his back smoking and she is fixing her make-up (further along on the same sofa), both classic post-sex signifiers. The ellipsis has been straightforwardly interpreted as the period of sexual intercourse, necessarily omitted for censorship reasons. Yet, it also indicates displacement. The camera backs away from them on the sofa before the image dissolves, and then moves towards Walter in the insurance office giving his (later) narration into Keyes's Dictaphone. This movement represents the retreat from the couple and their coupling, and the substitution of Walter, all alone, satisfying himself with exposition and explanation. After waiting while he speaks, the camera pulls back; the film is now ready to return to them in the apartment. They may have had sex, but there is the suggestion that they have not, and her tears are the reason for the reapplication of make-up. This suggestion does not merely act as a disguise for the sex that cannot be shown, but helps create the sense, as they sit at each end of the sofa, strangely disconnected, that to all intents and purposes, *it did not happen*. This is the hole at the heart of the film that Stanwyck's performance occupies, but is mindful never to fill.

Stanwyck does not only present the opaque female who, for whatever reason, can only hint at a hidden inner self. She presents something more amorphous or nebulous. Despite the hard exterior, Phyllis is not the finished article. Bronfen writes that she has 'no unequivocal meaning', and draws attention to a series of close-ups of Phyllis in the film where '[w]e must look at her, and then, because we never see the object her thoughts are directed at, we follow her gaze into an abstract realm' (114, 110). This is especially marked in one of the supermarket scenes when Walter walks brusquely away from her, and the end of the scene is delayed as she stands still, and stares out, into some strange nowhere space, wide-eyed, with a zombie-like expression (as agitated music plays on the soundtrack). She is perturbed by Walter's behaviour, but the heightening and her peculiarity declare a special significance that is not revealed. The film does not show Walter murdering the husband in the front passenger seat of the car. This takes place off-screen and instead the camera locks on to Phyllis who sits in the driver's seat, her largely impassive face staring ahead. The husband is resisting and wriggling as he dies, and he is disturbing her chair, but this draws attention to the stillness of her head and body, and the extent to which she is unmoved. This could be straightforwardly interpreted as stone cold ruthlessness, but it appears to be something less determined. As her eyes, unblinking, stare straight ahead, her expression is unformed, virtually gormless. She makes the slightest of movements, straightening her head, and tightening her face, only a little, by tucking in her chin and closing her mouth. Only at the end of the shot does a smile seem to be

coming into view but this looks to be part of a mask, equally
dislocated and unrevealing, and as the smile forms, the image is
dissolving. It is important to stress, at this decisive and critical
occasion in the film, as we experience the murder through her, how
indefinite Stanwyck's minimalism is.

Her lack of definition gives the film an instability, something
profoundly ungraspable at its heart. This internally disturbs that
'neat' and careful structure that Farber and Agee disliked (and, like
the fetish, this necessary imperfection maintains the film's allure).
When Phyllis reveals her history on his sofa, and half her face is in
shadow, the lighting is precisely what one might expect for the
shadowy, duplicitous 'enigmatic' 'femme fatale' existing on the
threshold of darkness. We are also shown a figure not fully formed,
betraying the artificiality and contrivance of that hard shell. Her
identity seems to be conjured as she goes along (with the plan). One
of the persistent patterns of the film is Walter – the salesman –

putting ideas into her head. She begins the film in a state of undress, and finishes her dressing and make-up in front of him and us; to rid herself of the husband, she presents herself to be made. The plan's formulation is simultaneous with Phyllis's formation. A problem with the wicked 'femme fatale' tag is that it is too much a static conception, and casts Phyllis as manipulator rather than open to manipulation. Stanwyck's performance does not act out a pre-conceived role, but presents a character in process, impressionable, and this susceptibility is in productive tension with the overriding tenor of restraint. As she is about to leave his apartment, he squeezes her upper arm and he opens the door with his other hand. The light from the hallway is cast on her face as the spell is cast on her. She is hypnotised: slow, and low, halting, she repeats his words, 'straight down the line'. He instructs and constructs, and she follows orders – she phones to tell him that, 'It's wonderful, Walter … just the way you wanted it'. Just the way *he* wanted it. Evans points out how Walter continually calls her 'Baby', and subtitles his essay 'Bringing up Baby'. She has replaced one dominating (older) man with another (younger) one. With the exception of the speeding exchange, the men have most of the clever lines and she rarely speaks more than she has to. Another aspect to the Stanwyck performance (and the male fantasy) is the apparently strong woman who is nevertheless obedient.

In the final scene between them in the Dietrichson house, near the end of the film, Walter's anxiety is expressed not only through loquaciousness but also through desperately spinning schemes, even when the game is lost. She stays in her chair quietly denying most of his accusations, but he says, '*Save it, I'm telling this*' because he is always 'telling' it – he tells the film. In this scene, Phyllis is languid *and* rigid: she sits deep in the chair (gun under the cushion) and waits, legs crossed, head fixed, hand with cigarette suspended in front of her face, in her white death shroud. This behaviour is implicit and incomplete enough to be interpreted as *her* clinical determination,

but it is also biding and fatalistic, necessarily so, because he determines her. There is a famous moment of suspense in the film that crystallises Phyllis's predicament, and distils the qualities of the Stanwyck performance. Keyes is in the hallway outside Walter's apartment expressing his suspicions about Mrs Dietrichson. Phyllis, in order not to be discovered visiting Walter, hides behind Walter's front door (unusually, the door opens outwards into the hallway) and outstretches her arm to hold the handle (so the door is not closed to reveal her). Hiding, held back, taut, silenced, and trapped, she is present but also absent, and concocted from the talk of others.

At the end of the film, Phyllis declares to Walter that she is 'rotten to the heart', incapable of love, and that she has used him. 'I never loved you Walter, not you or anybody else', she says. This might be the proof at last that she is the despicable 'femme fatale'. The status of these lines is difficult to ascertain, though, because of Stanwyck's complex and undemonstrative portrayal throughout the film. They could be the male projection speaking, just what Walter needs to hear: she must not love because love tames, sentimentalises, and disallows sex that transgresses. They could indicate a pitiless judgement on herself, a piece of masochism, or perhaps that no man was worth loving. A straightforward assessment of her becomes even more difficult when shortly afterwards she makes a desperate, apparently contradictory, demand, in one of her only moments of release, for Walter to hold her close. As she cries and plunges her head into his chest, the force of the performer's eruption is enhanced by the intensifying and emoting music, loud on the soundtrack, cascading. Equally, the music is justified as she moves from severe circumspection to fervour, suddenly rousing after being still for so long. She receives two bullets in her stomach as they embrace, but the surface had broken even before the bullets entered her. Stanwyck performs the demand as a shocking compulsion rather than as a recognition, or redemption. The latter options would make Phyllis more acceptable or forgivable, and would encourage the sort of simplistic assessment that Stanwyck's performance has been resisting. Her Phyllis Dietrichson is a woman of many possibilities – projected male fantasy, 'femme fatale', victim of social rules and gender roles, autonomous personality – none of them forcefully presented or fully realised.

5 STILLNESS

ALL I DESIRE (1953)
THERE'S ALWAYS TOMORROW (1956)

All I Desire (1953) and *There's Always Tomorrow* (1956) may be considered companion films: both were made in the 1950s in black and white, directed by Douglas Sirk, and star Barbara Stanwyck in her late forties, giving two of the best performances of her later period. In both, Stanwyck plays a middle-aged 'career' woman who 'returns'. In *All I Desire*, she is Naomi Murdoch, a less than successful actress, now playing music hall instead of 'legit' theatre. She returns to the small town of Riverdale where her family resides. (It is not clarified whether she left to pursue her career or to avoid scandal or a combination of both.) In *There's Always Tomorrow*, she is Norma Vale, a successful fashion designer. She returns to Clifford Groves, played by Fred MacMurray, a man whom she once worked for, and never stopped loving. Both contain families with a number of children of different ages: in *All I Desire*, her own, and in *There's Always Tomorrow*, Clifford's (he is married to Marion, played by Joan Bennett). The films explore the effects on Naomi and Norma, and on the interactions of both families.

Most commentaries understand the films, as most Sirk films are understood, to be ironic and subversive studies. On the surface, they appear to be conventional melodramas, tearjerkers or women's films, but they are actually interrogating society's conventionality. As Jeanine Basinger writes, 'He turned his films, which were made of the stuff of ordinary people's dreams, into complex portraits of a society build [sic] on materialism, false values, illusions, surfaces, romantic myths, blindness' (1977/8: 19). The family melodrama could be taken at face value or could be understood as a sly commentary on American bourgeois life in the 1950s. This social critique is one important aspect of Sirk's films, but it has become a default position and catch-all interpretation. For example, when Naomi first arrives back in her home town of Riverdale, a close-up shows her tears welling as she approaches her old home, and Dan Callahan writes, 'the Sirkian irony is particularly brutal here, for Naomi is looking with such longing at a house that all but broadcasts a sense of complacent, prison-like security' (2012: 181). There is, perhaps, a little too much 'security' in the interpretation too, because the home is not only a 'prison-like' place, but one of care and love, and the glowing windows in the darkness, also 'broadcast' cosiness, safety and warmth. It is a place of comfort *and* confinement. Inside and outside are competing seductions, and if there is anything 'brutal' here it is the unavoidable and unforgiving reminder of the life she did not live.

This tension gives us a different conception of irony, one that is close to that put by John Flaus with regard to Sirk (Flaus and Martin 2006), and one associated with New Criticism. T.S. Eliot saw irony as a sort of 'wit' where in dealing with any one kind of experience there is a recognition of the other kinds of experience that are possible (Abrams 1993 [1957]: 100). I.A. Richards defined irony in poetry as the equilibrium of opposing attitudes and evaluations (Abrams: 100). For Tag Gallagher, social critique is a commonplace feature of artworks, and does not explain the distinction of Sirk's films (1998). The achievement rests in the way they give physical expression to emotional dilemmas. Both Sirk films under discussion are about a woman trying to fit in, and about the ways in which she does and does not, and can and cannot, do this. She is on a cusp, and Stanwyck is ideal here because, as we have seen in her other films, she embodies the independence versus integration predicament.

According to this account, the viewer is caught up in the dilemmas, whereas the traditional ironic position may be a refuge from the emotionalism of 'popular' forms and offer a place of comfortable superiority (so that we are unwittingly complicit in bourgeois complacency). For Gallagher, the films refuse a safe distance and instead draw us towards ineluctable energies. Sirk reveals his own responsiveness: '[Y]ou have to take it from the people. And from the set ... An actor on a set is in a completely different position from what you can imagine ahead of time ... you have to take it from the last word, the last gesture ... you are building instinctively, even musically' (Harvey 2001: 392). The films are musical dramas, *melo*dramas, where the 'people' and the 'set' play off each other. They are involved. Gallagher mentions the 'framings and reframings' of Sirk's camera (18), and the theme of fitting in is explored stylistically by figures being brought in, or being left out of, the frame. Before we see Naomi's face and tears as she approaches the house, we see her large shadow extending along the sidewalk. The theatrical, larger-than-life figure intrudes into the domestic space of the small town. This shadow is too big, and the camera must retreat so that it can encompass it and her. It then leaves Naomi standing by the gate and moves up to take in the façade of the house, which fills the frame, and overwhelms. The film cuts back to her, and she is now walking directly towards the house, and towards the camera, into close-up, her eyes surveying her old home, *trying to take it in.* The face of the house and the face of the character are paired and both signify, without adequately expressing, emotional intensity. The close-up frame gives some equivalence to their vastly different sizes while also highlighting the problem of compatibility. How will they be brought together?

Accompanied by flooding strings on the soundtrack, this is a stirring experience for Naomi, but her approach to the house is steady. She is held upright by the formal Edwardian dress, and the tight frame is also constraining. From now on, her behaviour will be circumscribed, and she will have little room to manoeuvre (her rogue tear must be quickly wiped away as she snatches herself from the frame). At the point when she is closest to the camera, and the music crescendos, she stops, and stands still. Sirk said of Stanwyck, 'there is such an amazing tragic stillness about her' (Harvey: 390). Stillness is familiar as a blanket performance style in period dramas and goes with the generic territory, but for Stanwyck it is not a manner or an external imposition but a going concern. It is precisely and locally motivated, and, as Sirk suggests, part of her being.

In this sequence, the emotive music contrasts to Stanwyck's restraint. Basinger writes of Stanwyck: 'An actress of complex signals, she is the physical embodiment of a Sirkian universe. Her surface is hard. Adorned with expensive clothes, jewels, and furs, she looks tough and capable. However, her soft and almost pleading eyes offer a different clue to her inner state' (17). Stanwyck suggests more 'inner state' than some of Sirk's other leading actors, most famously Rock Hudson, with, as Harvey describes, their 'fundamental imperturbabilities, the unyielding depthlessness' (393). Her presence in fact brought contrast to the 'Sirkian universe', and worked well with the drama of her characters not quite fitting in. Her performances in both films are relatively nuanced (as is MacMurray's performance in *There's Always Tomorrow*) and are different in kind to those of the children in both films, even the older children, which are patent, even simplistic. Flaus talks about the way the implicit and explicit play off each other in Sirk's films. This may also be conceived as the subtle and less subtle taunting each other. Stanwyck even sustains the tension within her own performances, especially that of Naomi: suggestive and straightforward, capable of inference and forthright outburst.

I have elsewhere highlighted the fluency of movement in Hollywood performances (Klevan 2012), but stillness is a quality equally worth appreciating, and the two are related. (A person is never completely still, of course, so when I note the quality, I am referring to predominant, or relative, stillness, or the achievement of a still effect.) One way in which Stanwyck and Sirk make stillness effective is by contrasting it to, or setting it off against, movement (her own, other performers or the camera). This is not simply a formal achievement, but a way of rhythmically controlling and channelling the currents of emotion and meaning. After approaching the house, Naomi stands in the porch area, looks all around, rotates her body and, as she turns to see the hanging flower basket, her head stops still. Of significance is not simply the final, still position of the head, but it becoming still: the effect of stilling. (Her picking the key from the basket and the camera tilting to accommodate her movement – another slight, almost imperceptible, reframing – is sensitively discussed, in relation to our understanding the concept of a fictional world, by V.F. Perkins (2005: 28–33).)

A notable instance of this stilling effect is when she finally shows herself to the family at the doorway. One of the reasons her stillness is striking is that it interrupts a flurry of tightly knit, overlapping interactions between the family members. This intertwining takes place in one take. Lily, the middle daughter (Lori Nelson), moves around the back of her seated father, Henry (Richard Carlson), to Ted, the youngest son (Billy Gray), who pushes out from the landing above, through the banisters, to tease his sister. This brings in the eldest daughter, Joyce (Marcia Henderson) at the left of the frame who calls off-screen, across her father, to the housekeeper Lena (Lotte Stein). Ted joins the family at the table and, as he is moving to his seat, Henry rebukes his son just before Lena enters. Although the figures move in different planes, depth is reduced and the organisation is compact so they all seem close to the small dining room table (even Ted on the landing); and although the family are moving in different directions, and are more or less at odds, the dense blocking and the inclusive camera movements bring them together. Lena moves around the table and, as she begins to serve the food, she catches sight of Naomi. The film now cuts to show Naomi standing at

the doorway – alone. Her still separateness is stressed by coming
immediately after the family's interlocking movement. The music
rises to an intense pitch, but it does not come to a halt, as one might
expect, at the sight of Naomi, but continues to play over her as she
says, warmly and deliberately, 'Hello Lena'. (The stately, yet slightly
gravelly, vocal resonance of the later films may be contrasted with the
thinner, edgier, snap of the early films. Rather like a singer with a long
career, such as Frank Sinatra, Stanwyck takes advantage, through
modulating pitch, pace, volume and timbre, of the maturing voice,
and changing technologies.) Her address has a serenity that might
calm the music and the momentousness. Yet this is a star appearance
– the gauze of the inner door handily providing her with soft focus –
and bound to make waves. It sets in train a rhythmic sequence of stop
(Henry and Joyce staring, music concluding, the crash of cutlery),
move (Joyce's head turning to Henry, Henry rising), stop (Henry
standing), move (Lily rising and excitedly running towards her

mother, Ted's head turning in the foreground), stop (Ted's head coming to rest). Naomi's entrance in *All I Desire* exhibits some of Sirk's finest choreography of actors and camera, and although most of the achievement lies in the orchestration rather than in the acting – as far as one is able to make such a distinction given the close association – Stanwyck's stable presence anchors the design.

Nevertheless, the situation is unstable, and Naomi will need to hold herself together. Lily, the daughter who idolises her and wants to follow her example, helps by pulling her in, and squeezes both upper arms to hold Naomi in place. This gives Lily a good view and stops her mother getting away. Naomi then approaches Henry to shake his hand. Her eagerness is unreserved, but the formality of the handshake is poignant: after all, this was a man with whom she once shared a bed. The formality might at least keep the peace while this fraught meeting is negotiated. Naomi does not offer her hand at the last moment, but moves towards him with it outstretched.

Emphasising the straightness of her arm by prolonging the gesture also shows resolve and gives the impression that she is being straight. Already a somewhat inflexible figure, Henry further solidifies in shock and strains at civility: 'At any rate it was nice of you to come. I hope you enjoy Lily's play'. Right on the back of his words, she curtly exclaims 'Thank you, Henry', and even this fleeting retort shows Stanwyck's skill with ambivalence as Naomi is mocking his formality and usefully sustaining it (a little later she thanks him for 'not making a scene' on her arrival).

In both Sirk films, on a number of occasions, Stanwyck holds her arms, slightly away from her body, in a position of suspension. After touching Lily's face, Naomi keeps her gloved hand hovering by it. Joyce, hostile towards her mother because of her desertion, and generally disapproving of her character, backs off from her greeting; Naomi's arm hangs in the air, reverberating with the rejection. In *There's Always Tomorrow*, Norma removes Clifford's apron by spinning him around and then holding it out to him. As he fetches it from her and moves away towards the kitchen, her arm is left floating. It expresses her longing for him, or the domestic life, or something less definite: that she is left behind, or caught between, or

simply arrested by their uncanny reunion (Klevan 2005: 60–1). In *All I Desire*, at the party back at the Murdoch house, after Lily's school play, Sarah, the schoolteacher who has directed the play, and who is in love with Henry, arrives, and Naomi is keen to be warmly accepting and unthreatening. When Henry guides Sarah away to get a drink, Naomi is left eagerly wishing to say more to her and so she moves to follow them and extends her arms. People move away, and moments cannot be completed: much is left unsaid after engagements all too brief. She pulls her arms back, but they remain in a limbo position, stiffly held at right angles by her side. The danger of these gestures is that they will be held too long and look stilted, but Stanwyck manages to hold them longer than strictly necessary, but not long enough for them to lose their charge. This may be because she is communicating the period of abeyance expressionistically: in terms of her characters' feelings as they are drawn towards another but left behind (and, as we have seen, Stanwyck's characters are often left behind in her melodramas). She may also have a good feeling for dramatic time rather than real time – something that may vary from film to film, and context to context – specifically in this case the time during which the performer is allowed artificially to display something to the camera (and to us) without it becoming untenably demonstrative. In this instance, the film rescues her just in time. Her arms remain suspended while the 'Yale Boy' nervously asks her to dance. With a joyful friendliness, and without patronising, she says 'I'd love to' and they now rise up to fold around his neck. Seemingly frozen forlornly, her arms are reconceived as ready and waiting (as the film, elegantly and amusingly, conjoins disparate engagements). And, as she bursts into dance, stillness is reconceived as potential energy.

Stanwyck often sets off stillness against vigorous bursts. One achievement in performance is to restrain energy, then release it, and then restrain it again, without appearing to be repetitive, or simply yo-yoing. Shortly after her arrival, when Dutch (Lyle Bettger), a man who Naomi met illicitly by the lake in Riverdale as a young woman, is mentioned, she is stunned for an instant, but snaps out of it, and turns her body, with verve, to address everyone: 'Oh it's so good to see you all'. In both films, Naomi and Norma make a generous move when they wish to avoid an issue, but the assertion of comradeship compensates as well as evades. It also redeems, because it creates energy that prevents situations from congealing (and, once again, Stanwyck nuances matters of sincerity). Naomi also does the reverse, and abruptly breaks off generous acknowledgements a touch quicker than expected. A little later in the kitchen, she thanks Lena for staying in touch over the years and providing news of the family, and for 'everything' else, but she does not dwell on her thank-you – striking because we know she can dwell – or make it stick. Instead, she is already turning, and pulling away distractedly, excited to see all the old familiar things in the kitchen. As she enthusiastically approaches different furniture and objects in the kitchen – the 'old rocker' and the matchbox on the wall – the camera moves with her to bring these things into the shot (more reframing). Her energy seems to shape a space that does not simply exist but is brought into existence by her movements, brought into the drama: *dramatised*. Michael Walker persuasively argues that although Naomi's energy, sexual and otherwise, can be intimidating – observe the faces of Joyce and Henry as she embraces both Joyce's fiancé Russ and the 'Bunny Hug' with gusto – it ultimately revitalises the family (1990). Similarly, although somewhat less positively, Gallagher thinks that Sirk's films contain characters with strong wills that vitalise but also destroy, and which are rarely satisfied (life is masochism). For Gallagher, will can impose blindness or faith on things in ways that can make things better or worse. We often think of décor, especially in melodrama, disclosing meaning that the performers, or their characters, cannot express, or surrounding them with meanings, but he thinks instead that performers *give* symbolic force *to* the décor (19). Even though this sequence in the kitchen seems relatively insignificant, Stanwyck imbues it with tensions. Naomi is beneficently responsive and wishes to (re)integrate. She is also impulsive, which is vital and energising, but threatening to others, and shows an inability to settle. These are also characteristics of other Stanwyck performances, and one of the fascinations of a 'star system', in or out of Hollywood, is watching similar characteristics differently framed and inflected, in a variety of generic, narrative, and authorial contexts, which are themselves adjusting over time. In both the Sirk films, her characters yearn for the domestic but their energies disrupt its fulfilment.

Her energy is also put in tension with the stillness of others. So when Naomi vibrantly high-kicks the matchbox, in showgirl fashion, Joyce, entering the room at the wrong time, is assaulted by a shower of matches, and stopped in her tracks. This goes along with a pattern of interruption in the film where, rather than incidents discretely following each other, new ingredients cut in before the existing action is 'finished'. These interruptions feel like reverberations from the original disturbance, which is Naomi's arrival in Riverdale (and more specifically her arrival at the house where the family's reactions are like ripples). Equally, Stanwyck's stillness is in tension with the energy of others. There is a scene in *There's Always Tomorrow* where Norma, having been invited round to have dinner with Cliff and his family, sits upright and correct, as a couple of the children, who are offended by her presence, and her relationship with their father, rudely disrupt the dinner. Compositional harmony is disrupted too, and even before the children start leaving their seats, and moving around and away from the table, the film, with pans and cuts, tries to hold the party together. Unable to settle on a stable arrangement, the readjustments are effortful and ad hoc. Tall candles and candlesticks dissect and divide differently from shot to shot. Norma is particularly rigid in this scene, keeping her arms firmly by her side, moving mostly from the neck upwards, and rotating her head when she addresses a member of the family. Etiquette, self-protection, and the

desire not to assert, impose or enter inappropriately into the fray, all
account for her limitations in movement. The scene is a tussle
between decorum and the breaking of it. Once again, Stanwyck's
fixity is its focal point, but the film suitably does not find a way of
accommodating Norma *and* the family. In a later scene in *All I Desire*,
Sarah explains to Naomi that Henry loves her, and she should stay
with the family, but Naomi explains that there are too many
obstacles. Sarah says, 'Are you afraid, Naomi?' Naomi, who has been
walking away from Sarah (and the camera), responds by turning very
sharply to face her. She looks aghast, and freezes (like Lot's wife
turning into a pillar of salt). She appears indignant at the
impertinence of the suggestion *and* consumed by its revelatory force.
As Naomi turns, Joyce, sexually liberated by a wild horse ride with
Russ, hair released, bursts in through the front door at the back of
the frame, and rushes past her transfixed mother (all the way into
Sarah's arms). The decision to interrupt is risky because it may

distract from Naomi's astonishment. In fact, Joyce's dart past Naomi, whose body and eye-line remain set, accentuates the immobility and abnormality, and vividly shows that Naomi is, for better or for worse, overtaken by the vicissitudes of family.

One can see from these examples that the architecture of the family home is crucial to choreographing the relations. As Amy Lawrence writes in relation to *There's Always Tomorrow* and *The Reckless Moment* (1949), 'the pressures of the family are made visible in the structure of the house itself ... Each house seems to have an open floor plan, but the openness proves illusory, confining ... the staircase is often the site of crisis, frustration, and the incomplete trajectories that enact the hesitation between demands of family and one's own desires' (1999: 151, 157). The house in *All I Desire* has a particularly elaborate staircase in that its lower portion divides with routes off to both the kitchen at the back and living area at the front creating an intersection of three routes (upstairs, kitchen, downstairs living area). After Naomi's scene in the kitchen with Lena, her first encounter with Henry is set in this in-between space. The landing divides, and splits, testing Naomi's comportment, and amply illustrates Stanwyck's ability to vary the use of stillness. At first, as Henry attacks her claiming that 'years of desertion' cannot be exchanged for a 'few minutes of charm', her sturdy stance is a shield. Then, as he confronts her and comes face to face, and she shouts back, it establishes firm foundations, a refusal to cede ground, a position of strength. She 'spit[s] out the words as fast and contemptuously as possible' (Callahan: 181), her scolding delivery a reminder of the performer's excoriating, pre-Code rages, and the challenge is not to collapse her posture given the speed and the scorn. Lena enters below and shouts up (intentionally to interrupt their argument), and Naomi's unyielding defiance now appears as guilt and embarrassment; she is exposed, caught in the act. A little later, and further down the stairs, she rests her back against the wall, which gives her support and keeps her straight. She requests an accord, if only for the children's sake and, reaching out tentatively, her fingertips delicately touch the edge of his waistcoat. She holds her arm in this position for as much as twenty seconds (during which he turns slightly so that the position of her hand is more evident). Holding in this way is precarious. When he attacks her verbally again, she pulls away and scurries off up the stairs. The woman fleeing in distress, alarm or anger, while lifting up her dress, is a familiar sight in costume dramas, but coming after Naomi's careful, and caring, gesture – the hasty retreat contrasting to the sustained placement – it is poignant.

With its exits and entrances, the landing is a stage in this house that is a theatre. The most explicit performance in the house takes place on, and by, this same landing, at the party, when Naomi, after being urged by Lily, reads a love poem by Elizabeth Barrett Browning (more precisely, sonnet 43 from *Sonnets from the Portuguese*, 1850). Controlling her visibility, she first turns down the 'house lights', begins her reading in the shadows, and then moves halfway down the stairs. From then on, Naomi stays put, but she does not merely stand and stay still. She projects stillness. The audience is assembled: Lena emerges to watch through the kitchen doorway, while the rest of the guests gather around the staircase in the lounge. Charles Affron is particularly interested in occasions such as this poetry reading where '[t]he validation of on-screen performance by the approving glance of an on-screen viewer, a frequent device of cinematic self-reflexivity, becomes a sign of affect when that viewer also has a specifically personal relationship with the performer' (1982: 140). Here, shots of Henry, Sarah and Lily, all with a 'specifically personal relationship with the performer', show them watching Naomi's performance. Affron goes on to say that 'we are often disappointed by the nonmusical "numbers" performed in films … [they] are unconvincing proofs of the acting ability demonstrated elsewhere in these films' and he cites this section from *All I Desire* as one of his examples (140). However, leaving aside that such moments could be precisely about the overestimation of the on-screen viewer (for example, on this occasion, Lily), Naomi's reading could never be a convincing proof of 'acting ability' because of its tangled status. Stanwyck, the good film performer, is playing a character who may or may not be a good performer, *and* who may or may not be a good Actress of 'legitimate' theatre. The character is also giving a particular type of performance at a party, to friends and family, which has its own standards. Various genres of performance are in the mix for Stanwyck – film melodrama, theatrical chamber drama, and poetry reading – all with their own criteria. Cinema and theatre merge as features of film, such as close-up, or quietness of voice, are combined with live performance. Furthermore, professional and domestic roles are simultaneously enacted. Stanwyck is performing Naomi who is performing many things that she wishes to bring to life: the sonnet, the famous actress, the mother, the wife and the lover.

Molly Haskell writes, 'The actress ... is a key female figure throughout film history ... the actress merely extends the role-playing dimension of woman, emphasizing what she already is ... A woman plays roles naturally in self-defense ... She adopts masks and plays roles that will enable her to stall for time, stand back, watch, intuit, react ... But she also plays roles, adapts to others, "aims to please"' (1987 [1973]: 242–3). 'The actress' is yet another of Stanwyck's roles which complicate the boundaries of sincerity. Her reading of this popular love sonnet balances the need to exploit and, at the same time, justify the sentiment. Her delivery is performed, but not proclaimed. It is communicative and easy, but not too colloquial or coarse. It is dignified, but not beyond an improper suggestion (Callahan writes that she 'opens her mouth and lets her tongue flutter near her teeth on the "th" sound in "death," so that it sounds almost lascivious' (182)). It is dulcet, and soothing, but not too mellifluous or honeyed. It is fluent, but studiously outlines the metre and scan of the verse. It is emotive, but her own emotions are

not indulged, as she prefers to emphasise the voice of the sonnet. It is
addressed, to Henry in particular, but not pointed (someone else, the
poet perhaps, is making the points). Despite all the aspects in play,
she uses the poetry to gather them to a position of security, and
harmonise them: to put the ambivalences into equilibrium.

Naomi, like Norma Vale, reaches out while holding back. When
Naomi steps out of the shadows and moves to the edge of the
staircase, she makes herself visible and makes the crowd more visible
to her. The reading of the poetry book presents opportunities for
looking up and down, and controlling eye contact. Eye movement
and other slight head movements become striking when the body is
largely still. There is a close-up of her face on the line, 'I love thee
with a love I seemed to lose/With my lost saints', and she looks up on
'seemed to lose' (and makes a slight shake of her head), emphasising
a phrase that is pertinent to her own situation. Stanwyck's eye
variations are particularly complex during Norma's interactions with
Clifford in *There's Always Tomorrow*. At the beginning of the film,
Norma has arrived at Clifford Grove's home unexpectedly, where he
is all alone after being deserted for the evening by his family. The
film concerns his neglect and the possible salvation, ultimately
unfulfilled, offered to him by Norma, and the ambiguity surrounding
her ambitions and motivations (see Klevan 2005: 53–63 for an
analysis of the opening fifteen minutes of the film). They go to a
show together and they talk in the interval. Because they are seated
adjacently, on a row, rather than facing, the actors must make an
effort to turn towards each other and, equally, can sensibly look
away. They also each hold a programme that provides, like the
reading of the poetry book, a justifiable excuse to redirect the eyes.
With her eyes down, Norma says 'Are your offices far from here?',
then she looks up, her head slightly turned towards the camera, and
looks out, for a beat, before flicking her eyes towards him – and then
down again (her accentuated eyelashes embolden the movement).
Although each head and eye movement is noticeable, my delineating

makes them sound a little too marked, and discrete. Stanwyck times them to follow each other closely enough: executed with a touch more deliberateness and they would look too clearly contrived by the character (or indicate ponderous performing by the actress). As it stands, they look spontaneously in tune with the character's thought and feeling while the conscious manipulation by Norma of her gaze cannot be discounted. When she says, 'Why don't you ask me to skip the second act?', she stares right at him and the film cuts away before she blinks. Stanwyck shows that she can keep her eyes still too if need be. Throughout the film, Norma Vale's concentrated gaze at Cliff is admiring, inspecting, dissimulating, and calculated to capture his attention.

This directing and redirecting is true also of her larger movements and they convey the character's desire to confront and avoid. After the show, they go to visit Cliff's office-cum-showroom (he is a manufacturer of children's toys). Norma excitedly moves into the space. 'Oh what a wonderful display', she says with a little shriek on 'Oh', and it comes across as genuine *and* feigned, a touch too eager perhaps, as if he and the toys deserve an enthusiastic performance, one to which she is happily committed. When he responds with 'I hoped you'd like it', she stops and turns round to him sharply on the spot. There is a pattern in the film of her stopping and turning – alertly. Earlier, when Norma first arrives at his home, he opens the door and, because she is looking away, she is able to swivel on the spot to face him. She is slightly in shadow, he does not recognise her, and she waits a second or two before she walks forward towards him – into the light. A little later in the same scene, she walks into the main living area, with her back to the camera, before doing one of her swift turns. From this still position – her arms draped over the back of an armchair – she moves off again, deeper into the room, away from him and the camera. Then, after she admits that she intended to surprise him, he exclaims that, 'It's the nicest surprise I've had in years', and in response to his interest, she turns promptly to face him. Often, after addressing him directly, she quickly moves on. In the showroom, she says, 'Oh Cliff I'm so proud of you', but no sooner said, she is turning around and moving away, leaving no time for the significance of her admiration to be dwelt upon. She wants to make moments and quickly dissolve them.

Moving excitedly from toy to toy means that Norma escapes questions regarding herself – an adult playing with children's toys is a suitable image of avoidance and sublimation – while admiring him through his work. Sometimes she will hold on to something longer than necessary. She picks up Rex, the Walky-Talky Robot Man, and stares at him lovingly ('Oh I adore *him*', she says, emphasising 'him', rather than '*adore*', which sounds less affected, and draws attention to the robot – 'him' – rather than her own adoration). Cliff encourages her to carry on looking around, but she stays facing the robot, lost in wonder. She moves out of positions quicker than expected, or stays in them slightly longer, an arresting rhythm, like a jazz musician missing, or playing off, the formal beats. This would appear contrived were her time keeping not in keeping with the particular instance. He asks her to tell him why she quit her job as his designer without even a week's notice and, perturbed, she stops walking on, although she continues to stroke the head of a soft toy elephant. 'I had my reasons', she says, and moves to replace the elephant but, as if caught in the memory, she holds it a few inches above the table. And *then,* as she places it down, she changes the subject: 'Now … when am I going to meet Marion and the children?'. Stanwyck's little delay is eloquent, but it would be hackneyed were it not part of an elaborate pattern of respite and propulsion.

They approach the street organ, which they had invented together, and which becomes the focal object of the scene. Perhaps content now to limit her room for manoeuvre, she nestles in between a post behind her and the organ in front of her – there is just enough space for her to fit – and she stands there for the rest of the exchange.

She controls the release of the past to re-forge their relationship in the present, and this is conducted by the movement of her hand. 'Oh I remember it so clearly', she says, and places both hands on the organ lovingly. As she remembers different aspects, she points gently. Apparently in an effort to remember the tune being played by the 'little old Italian organ grinder', she drops her head, and raises her hand to her brow. It is unlikely Norma has forgotten but, even if she has, her dramatisation of trying to remember invites his involvement by allowing him to complete the memory, and allowing her to see whether he can. He has done more than remember, he has memorialised the tune as the organ's theme, and he turns the wheel to make it play. From now on, he is intimately involved in the retelling, and in the intimacy. Even though she removes her hand from her forehead as she raises her head and smiles, it remains in front of her face but below her chin (so that it does not cover her face). As she recalls the title – 'Blue Moon' – it drops away (out of the frame). The predominant composure of the body draws one's attention to the gesturing of arms (and eyes). With its fond reminiscences, regrets and matters left unspoken, the scene could have been too loosely sentimental. Without removing the sentiment, or adopting an ironic point of view, Stanwyck's suspensions and accentuations provide unexpected tensile strength and create undercurrents. There is a honing and a slight stiffening of movements which remain natural enough. Carefulness of gesture is more prevalent in her later films, and is particularly well deployed in *All I Desire* and *There's Always Tomorrow*, perhaps because it is at home in the 'Sirkian universe'. It is another technique Stanwyck uses to trouble one's assessment of the character (and their motives). Most film performances, even ostensibly naturalistic ones, are heightened and contrived, so should the calculation be attributed to the character or the performance? Performance is also a feature of everyday life and being, making authenticity even more difficult to gauge. The medium is itself poised between the natural and the artificial. Many films take advantage of it, but Stanwyck is particularly fine at locating the precise point of insecurity.

She is able to close the scene with a piece of behaviour that is artificially pronounced, and she can carry it off because it is embedded within the idiom that she has naturalised. At the end of the scene, Norma returns to the street organ and starts turning the handle. Stanwyck is positioned in relation to the organ so that her arm may stretch across it, and the profile of her body, and the extended arm, may be displayed for the camera. 'It's been a wonderful evening', Norma says and then, although she stops turning, she keeps her hand on the handle. She stares ahead, away into the distance, and the combination of the retention of her arm position and the unblinking persistence of her gaze make this a declaration of stillness. She then says an apposite line, in the low, smooth register of 'Hello Lena': 'You know, tonight, for a little while, time stood still'. She punctures the line with prolonged pauses, creating pockets of stillness in speech – 'You know [pause] tonight [long pause] for a little while [long pause] time stood still' – so that 'for a little while' she may hold on to the clauses (and what is conjured between them), and endeavour to arrest progression. Norma's posture, gesture and delivery are at their most affected, and yet her behaviour, although not transparent, seems a sincere expression of her emotion. This paradoxical quality is exemplary of the Stanwyck achievement.

A FINAL WORD

Barbara Stanwyck is one of the outstanding film stars, but she is particularly difficult to pin down. This is not only because she appeared in many genres, but because her performances are responsive, various and nuanced, and tend not to harden into a few definite features. Unlike so many of her companions in Hollywood – Jimmy Cagney, Humphrey Bogart, Katharine Hepburn, Bette Davis, Greta Garbo, Marlene Dietrich and more – she was, and is, rarely, if ever, impersonated by impressionists. She does not have a set of obvious mannerisms to be accentuated and caricatured. Her best roles, therefore, are ones where aspects of identity are at stake or where motivations are uncertain, and which incorporate role-playing. These include: 'party-girl' (*Ladies of Leisure*), preacher and faith-healer (*The Miracle Woman*), Mother (*Stella Dallas*), dissembling showgirl (*Ball of Fire*), con woman (*The Lady Eve*), fantasy figure (*Double Indemnity*), actress (*All I Desire*), and old flame (*There's Always Tomorrow*). These deceptive characters allowed her to complicate the boundaries between independence and dependence, sincerity and pretence, truth and falsity, serious and comic, straightforward and recessive, natural and unnatural, flexibility and fixity. Despite the ambivalence and ambiguity of her characters, Stanwyck's best performances are not wilfully obscure or loosely enigmatic, nor do they revel in perversity; and despite the complexity, they do not proclaim themselves as clever or demanding. Although these performances operate in an in-between place, they are sharp, distinct and potent.

BIBLIOGRAPHY

Abrams, M.H. (1993; orig. 1957) *A Glossary of Literary Terms*, Fort Worth: Harcourt Brace College Publishers.

Affron, C. (1977) *Star Acting: Gish, Garbo, Davis*, New York: E.P. Dutton.

Affron, C. (1982) *Cinema and Sentiment*, Chicago: University of Chicago Press.

Agee, J. (2000; orig. 1941–50, dates of individual essays provided in the text) *Agee on Film: Criticism and Comment on the Movies*, New York: Modern Library.

Basinger, J. (1977/8) '"The Lure of the Gilded Cage": *All I Desire* and *There's Always Tomorrow*', *Bright Lights Journal*, 6 (Winter): 17–19.

Borde, R. and Chaumeton, E. (2002; orig. 1955) *A Panorama of American Film Noir: 1941–1953*, San Francisco: City Light Books.

Britton, A. (1994) '*The Lady from Shanghai*', in I. Cameron (ed.), *The Movie Book of Film Noir*, London: Studio Vista, 213–21.

Britton, A. (1995; orig. 1984) *Katharine Hepburn: Star as Feminist*, London: Studio Vista.

Britton, A. (2009; orig. 1989) 'The Philosophy of the Pigeonhole: Wisconsin Formalism and "The Classical Style"', in *Britton on Film: The Complete Film Criticism of Andrew Britton*, Barry Keith Grant (ed.), Detroit: Wayne State University Press.

Bronfen, E. (2004) 'Femme Fatale: Negotiations of Tragic Desire', *New Literary History*, 35, 1 (Winter): 103–16.

Callahan, D. (2012) *Barbara Stanwyck: The Miracle Woman*, Jackson: University Press of Mississippi.

Capra, F. (1971) *The Name Above the Title: An Autobiography*, New York: Macmillan.

Carney, R. (1996; orig. 1986) *American Vision: The Films of Frank Capra*, Hanover and London: Wesleyan University Press.

Cavell, S. (1981) *Pursuits of Happiness: The Hollywood Comedy of Remarriage*, Cambridge, MA and London: Harvard University Press.

Cavell, S. (1996) *Contesting Tears: The Hollywood Melodrama of the Unknown Woman*, Chicago and London: The University of Chicago Press.

Cavell, S. (2004) *Cities of Words: Pedagogical Letters on a Register of the Moral Life*, Cambridge, MA and London: The Belknap Press of Harvard University Press.

Cohen, M.S. (1974) 'Film Noir: The Actor – Villains and Victims', *Film Comment*, 10, 6 (November/December): 27–9.

Cowie, E. (1993) 'Film Noir and Women', in J. Copjec (ed.), *Shades of Noir*, New York and London: Verso Books, 121–65.

DiBattista, M. (2001) *Fast-Talking Dames*, New Haven and London: Yale University Press.

Dickos, A. (2002) *Street With No Name: A History of the Classic American Film Noir*, Kentucky: The University Press of Kentucky.

DiOrio, A. (1984) *Barbara Stanwyck: A Biography*, New York: Coward-McCann.

Doane, M.A. (1982) 'Film and the Masquerade: Theorising the Female Spectator', *Screen*, 23, 3–4 (September/October): 74–87.

Doane, M.A. (1988) *The Desire to Desire: The Woman's Film of the 1940s*, Basingstoke and London: Macmillan.

Dyer, R. (1998; orig. 1979) *Stars*, London: British Film Institute.

Evans, P.W. (1994) '*Double Indemnity* (or Bringing Up Baby)', in I. Cameron (ed.), *The Movie Book of Film Noir*, London: Studio Vista, 165–73.

Farber, M. (2009; orig. 1942–77, dates of individual essays provided in the text) *Farber on Film: The Complete Writings of Manny Farber*, R. Polito (ed.), New York: The Library of America.

Fischer. L. (1999) 'Sirk and the Figure of the Actress: *All I Desire*', *Film Criticism*, 23, 2/3 (Winter): 136–49.

Flaus, J. and Martin, A. (2006) *There's Always Tomorrow*, DVD Commentary, Madmen Entertainment Pty Ltd.

Gallagher, B. (1987) '"I Love You Too": Sexual Warfare & Homoeroticism in Billy Wilder's *Double Indemnity*', *Literature/Film Quarterly*, 15, 4: 237–46.

Gallagher, T. (1998) 'White Melodrama: Douglas Sirk', *Film Comment*, 34, 6 (November/December): 16–27.

Gledhill, C. (1998; orig. 1978) '*Klute* 1 – A Contemporary Film Noir and Feminist Criticism' in E. A. Kaplan (ed.), *Women in Film Noir*, London: British Film Institute, 20–34.

Grossman, J. (2009) *Rethinking the Femme Fatale in Film Noir: Ready for Her Close-Up*, Basingstoke: Palgrave MacMillan.

Harvey, J. (1998; orig. 1987) *Romantic Comedy in Hollywood: From Lubitsch to Sturges*, New York: Da Capo Press.

Harvey, J. (2001) *Movie Love in the Fifties*, Cambridge, MA: Da Capo Press.

Harvey, S. (1981) 'The Strange Fate of Barbara Stanwyck', *Film Comment*, 17, 2 (March/April): 34–6.

Haskell, M. (1987; orig. 1973) *From Reverence to Rape: The Treatment of Women in the Movies*, Chicago and London: University of Chicago Press.

Hayward, S. (2006; orig. 1996) *Cinema Studies: The Key Concepts*, Oxford: Routledge.

Hirsch, F. (1981) *The Dark Side of the Screen: Film Noir*, Cambridge, MA: Da Capo Press.

Jameson, R.T. (1981) 'Stanwyck and Capra', *Film Comment*, 17, 2 (Mar/Apr): 37–9.

Johnston, C. (1998; orig. 1978) '*Double Indemnity*', in E. A. Kaplan (ed.), *Women in Film Noir*, London: British Film Institute, 89–98.

Kael, P. (1993; orig. 1982) *5001 Nights at the Movies*, London: Marion Boyars.

Kaplan, E.A. (2000; orig. 1983) 'The Case of the Missing Mother: Maternal Issues in Vidor's *Stella Dallas*' in E.A Kaplan (ed.), *Feminism and Film*, Oxford: Oxford University Press, 466–78.

Keser, R. (2005) '*Forbidden*', *Senses of Cinema*, 37. Available at: http://sensesofcinema.com/2005/cteq/forbidden/ (accessed 23rd May 2012).

Klevan, A. (2003) 'The Purpose of Plot and the Place of Joan Bennett in Fritz Lang's *The Woman in the Window*', *Cineaction*, 62: 15–21.

Klevan, A. (2005) *Film Performance: From Achievement to Appreciation*, London: Wallflower Press.

Klevan, A. (2012) 'Living Meaning: The Fluency of Film Performance' in A. Taylor (ed.), *Theorizing Film Acting*, London and New York: Routledge, 33–46.

Lane, A. (2007) 'Lady Be Good', *The New Yorker*. Available at: http://www.newyorker.com/reporting/2007/04/30/070430fa_fact_lane (accessed 23rd May 2012).

LaSalle, M. (2000) *Complicated Women: Sex and Power in Pre-Code Hollywood*, New York: Thomas Dunne Books.

Lawrence, A. (1999) 'Trapped in a Tomb of their Own Making: Max Ophüls's *The Reckless Moment* and Douglas Sirk's *There's Always Tomorrow*', *Film Criticism*, 23, 2/3 (Winter): 150–76.

Lesser, W. (1991) *His Other Half: Men Looking At Women Through Art*, Cambridge, MA and London England: Harvard University Press.

McBride, J. (2010) 'Capra Before He Became 'Capraesque'', *Sight and Sound*, 20, 12 (December): 44–9.

Madsen, A. (2001; orig. 1994) *Stanwyck*, Lincoln: iUniverse.com, Inc.

Manon, H. S. (2005) 'Some Like it Cold: Fetishism in Billy Wilder's *Double Indemnity*', *Cinema Journal*, 44, 4 (Summer): 18–43.

Mast, G. (1982) *Howard Hawks, Storyteller*, New York and Oxford: Oxford University Press.

Millar, G. (1980) 'Billy Wilder' in R. Roud (ed.), *Cinema: A Critical Dictionary – The Major Film-Makers*, London: Secker and Warburg, 1081–87.

Murphy, K. (1990) 'Farewell My Lovelies', *Film Comment*, 26, 4 (July), 33–8.

Naremore, J. (2008; orig. 1998) *More Than Night: Film Noir and its Contexts*, Berkeley, Los Angeles and London: University of California Press.

Nehme, F.S. (2007) 'Barbara Stanwyck: The Professional's Professional'. Available at: http://selfstyledsiren.blogspot.co.uk/2007/07/barbara-stanwyck-professionals.html (accessed 23rd May 2012).

Paris, J.A. (2004) '"Murder Can Sometimes Smell Like Honeysuckle": Billy
Wilder's *Double Indemnity* (1944)', in A. Silver and J. Ursini (eds), *Film
Noir Reader 4*, New Jersey: Limelight Editions, 8–23.

Perkins, V.F. (2005) 'Where is the World? The Horizon of Events in Movie
Fiction', in J. Gibbs and D. Pye (eds), *Style and Meaning: Studies in the
Detailed Analysis of Films*, Manchester: Manchester University Press, 16–41.

Place, J. (1998; orig. 1978) 'Women in Film Noir', in E. A. Kaplan (ed.),
Women in Film Noir, London: British Film Institute, 47–68.

Rabinovitz, P. (2002) *Black & White & Noir: America's Pulp Modernism*, New
York: Columbia University Press.

Rafferty, T. (2007) 'The Infinite Variety of Lady Stanwyck', *The New York
Times*. Available at http://query.nytimes.com/gst/fullpage.html?res=
9C04E6DD1E3FF931A15757C0A9619C8B63&pagewanted=all
(accessed 23rd May 2012).

Ray, R.B. (2008) *The ABCs of Classic Hollywood*, Oxford: Oxford University
Press.

Rothman, W. (2004; orig. 1988) *The 'I' of the Camera: Essays in Film Criticism,
History, and Aesthetics*, Cambridge: Cambridge University Press.

Sarris, A. (1985; orig. 1968) *The American Cinema: Directors and Directions
1929–1968*, Chicago: The University of Chicago Press.

Sarris, A. (1998) *'You Ain't Heard Nothin' Yet': The American Talking Film
History and Memory, 1927–1949*, Oxford: Oxford University Press.

Schickel, R. (1992) *Double Indemnity*, London: British Film Institute.

Singer, I. (2008) *Cinematic Mythmaking: Philosophy in Film*, Cambridge, MA
and London: The MIT Press.

Sipiora, P. (2011) 'Phenomenological Masking: Complications of Identity in
Double Indemnity', in K. McNally (ed.), *Billy Wilder, Movie-Maker: Critical
Essays on the Films*, Jefferson, NC and London: McFarland & Company,
Inc., 102–16.

Smith, E. (1974) *Starring Miss Barbara Stanwyck*, New York: Crown Publishers.

Stables, K. (1998; orig. 1978) 'The Postmodern Always Rings Twice:
Constructing the Femme Fatale in 1990s Cinema', in E. A. Kaplan (ed.),
Women in Film Noir, London: British Film Institute, 164–82.

Thomson, D. (1981) 'Stella Stanwyck', *Film Comment*, 17, 2 (March/April): 41–3.

Thomson, D. (1995; orig. 1975) *A Biographical Dictionary of Film*, London: André Deutsch.

Turner, D. (2006) 'The Interiority of the Unknown Woman', unpublished doctoral thesis, University of Kent, UK.

Tyler, P. (1971; orig. 1947) *Magic and Myth of the Movies*, London: Secker and Warburg.

Walker, M. (1990) 'All I Desire', *Movie*, 34/5 (Winter): 31–47.

Wayne, J.E. (2009) *The Lives and Loves of Barbara Stanwyck*, London: JR Books.

Williams, L. (1984) '"Something Else Besides a Mother": *Stella Dallas* and the Maternal Melodrama', *Cinema Journal*, 24, 1 (Fall): 2–27.

Wood, R. (2006; orig. 1968) *Howard Hawks*, Detroit: Wayne State University Press.

FILMOGRAPHY

Feature Films

BROADWAY NIGHTS (Joseph C. Boyle, USA, 1927), Fan dancer
(uncredited).

THE LOCKED DOOR (George Fitzmaurice, USA, 1929), Ann Carter.

MEXICALI ROSE (Erle C. Kenton, USA, 1929), Mexicali Rose.

LADIES OF LEISURE (Frank Capra, USA, 1930), Kay Arnold.

ILLICIT (Vincent Ives, USA, 1931), Anne Vincent.

TEN CENTS A DANCE (Lionel Barrymore, USA, 1931), Barbara O'Neill.

NIGHT NURSE (William A. Wellman, USA, 1931), Lora Hart.

THE STOLEN JOOLS (Short, Various, USA, 1931), Herself – Mrs. Frank
Fay.

THE MIRACLE WOMAN (Frank Capra, USA, 1931), Florence 'Faith'
Fallon.

FORBIDDEN (Frank Capra, USA, 1932), Lulu Smith.

SHOPWORN (Nicholas Grinde, USA, 1932), Kitty Lane.

SO BIG! (William A. Wellman, USA, 1932), Selina Peake De Jong.

THE PURCHASE PRICE (William A. Wellman, USA, 1932), Joan Gordon,
aka Francine La Rue.

THE BITTER TEA OF GENERAL YEN (Frank Capra, USA, 1933),
Megan Davis.

LADIES THEY TALK ABOUT (Howard Bretherton/William Keighley,
USA, 1933), Nan Taylor, alias of Nan Ellis, aka Mrs. Andrews.

BABY FACE (Alfred E. Green, USA, 1933), Lily Powers.

EVER IN MY HEART (Archie Mayo, USA, 1933), Mary Archer Wilbrandt.

GAMBLING LADY (Archie Mayo, USA, 1934), Lady Lee.

A LOST LADY (Alfred E. Green, USA, 1934), Marian Ormsby Forrester.

THE SECRET BRIDE (William Dieterle, USA, 1934), Ruth Vincent.

THE WOMAN IN RED (Robert Florey, USA, 1935), Shelby Barret Wyatt.

RED SALUTE (Sidney Lansfield, USA, 1935), Drue Van Allen.

ANNIE OAKLEY (George Stevens, USA, 1935), Annie Oakley.

A MESSAGE TO GARCIA (George Marshall, USA, 1936), Raphaelita Maderos.

THE BRIDE WALKS OUT (Leigh Jason, USA, 1936), Carolyn Martin.

HIS BROTHER'S WIFE (W. S. Van Dyke, USA, 1936), Rita Wilson Claybourne.

BANJO ON MY KNEE (John Cromwell, USA, 1936), Pearl Elliott Holley.

THE PLOUGH AND THE STARS (John Ford, USA, 1936), Nora Clitheroe.

INTERNES CAN'T TAKE MONEY (Alfred Santell, USA, 1937), Janet Haley.

THIS IS MY AFFAIR (William A. Seiter, USA, 1937), Lil Duryea.

STELLA DALLAS (King Vidor, USA, 1937), Stella Martin Dallas.

BREAKFAST FOR TWO (Alfred Santell, USA, 1937), Valentine 'Val' Ransome.

ALWAYS GOODBYE (Sidney Lansfield, USA, 1938), Margot Weston.

THE MAD MISS MANTON (Leigh Jason, USA, 1938), Melsa Manton.

UNION PACIFIC (Cecil B. DeMille, USA, 1939), Mollie Monahan.

GOLDEN BOY (Rouben Mamoulian, USA, 1939), Lorna Moon.

REMEMBER THE NIGHT (Mitchell Leisen, USA, 1940), Lee Leander.

THE LADY EVE (Preston Sturges, USA, 1941), Jean Harrington.

MEET JOHN DOE (Frank Capra, USA, 1941), Ann Mitchell.

YOU BELONG TO ME (Wesley Ruggles, USA, 1941), Dr. Helen Hunt.

BALL OF FIRE (Howard Hawks, USA, 1941), Katherine 'Sugarpuss' O'Shea.

THE GREAT MAN'S LADY (William A. Wellman, USA, 1942), Hannah Sempler.

THE GAY SISTERS (Irving Rapper, USA, 1942), Fiona Gaylord.

LADY OF BURLESQUE (William A. Wellman, USA, 1943), Deborah Hoople, aka Dixie Daisy.

FLESH AND FANTASY (Julien Duvivier, USA, 1943), Joan Stanley.

DOUBLE INDEMNITY (Billy Wilder, USA, 1944), Phyllis Dietrichson.

HOLLYWOOD CANTEEN (Delmer Daves, USA, 1944), Herself.

HOLLYWOOD VICTORY CARAVAN (William Russell, USA, 1945), Herself.

CHRISTMAS IN CONNECTICUT (Peter Godfrey, USA, 1945), Elizabeth Lane.

MY REPUTATION (Curtis Bernhardt, USA, 1946), Jessica Drummond.

THE BRIDE WORE BOOTS (Irving Pichel, USA, 1946), Sally Warren.

THE STRANGE LOVE OF MARTHA IVERS (Lewis Milestone, USA, 1946), Martha Ivers

CALIFORNIA (John Farrow, USA, 1946), Lily Bishop.

THE TWO MRS. CARROLLS (Peter Godfrey, USA, 1947), Sally Morton Carroll.

THE OTHER LOVE (André de Toth, USA, 1947), Karen Duncan.

CRY WOLF (Peter Godfrey, USA, 1947), Sandra Marshall.

VARIETY GIRL (George Marshall, USA, 1947), Herself.

B.F.'S DAUGHTER (Robert Z. Leonard, USA, 1948), Pauline 'Polly' Fulton Brett.

SORRY, WRONG NUMBER (Anatole Litvak, USA, 1948), Leona Stevenson

THE LADY GAMBLES (Michael Gordon, USA, 1949), Joan Phillips Boothe.

EAST SIDE, WEST SIDE (Mervyn LeRoy, USA, 1949), Jessie Bourne.

THE FILE ON THELMA JORDON (Robert Siodmak, USA, 1950), Thelma Jordon

NO MAN OF HER OWN (Mitchell Leisen, USA, 1950), Helen Ferguson/Patrice Harkness.

THE FURIES (Anthony Mann, USA, 1950), Vance Jeffords.

TO PLEASE A LADY (Clarence Brown, USA, 1950), Regina Forbes.

THE MAN WITH A CLOAK (Fletcher Markle, USA, 1951), Lorna
    Bounty.
CLASH BY NIGHT (Fritz Lang, USA, 1952), Mae Doyle D'Amato.
JEOPARDY (John Sturges, USA, 1953), Helen Stilwin.
TITANIC (Jean Negulesco, USA, 1953), Julia Sturges.
ALL I DESIRE (Douglas Sirk, USA, 1953), Naomi Murdoch.
THE MOONLIGHTER (Roy Rowland, USA, 1953), Rela.
BLOWING WILD (Hugo Fregonese, USA, 1953), Marina Conway.
WITNESS TO MURDER (Roy Rowland, USA, 1954), Cheryl Draper.
EXECUTIVE SUITE (Robert Wise, USA, 1954), Julia O. Tredway.
CATTLE QUEEN OF MONTANA (Allan Dwan, USA, 1954), Sierra
    Nevada Jones.
THE VIOLENT MEN (Rudolph Maté, USA, 1955), Martha Wilkison.
ESCAPE TO BURMA (Alan Dwan, USA, 1955), Gwen Moore.
THERE'S ALWAYS TOMORROW (Douglas Sirk, USA, 1956), Norma
    Miller Vale.
THE MAVERICK QUEEN (Joseph Kane, USA, 1956), Kit Banion.
THESE WILDER YEARS (Roy Rowland, USA, 1956), Ann Dempster.
CRIME OF PASSION (Gerd Oswald, USA, 1957), Kathy Ferguson Doyle.
TROOPER HOOK (Charles Marquis Warren, USA, 1957), Cora Sutliff.
FORTY GUNS (Samuel Fuller, USA, 1957), Jessica Drummond.
WALK ON THE WILD SIDE (Edward Dmytryk, USA, 1962), Jo
    Courtney.
ROUSTABOUT (John Rich, USA, 1964), Maggie Morgan.
THE NIGHT WALKER (William Castle, USA, 1964), Irene Trent.

Television

THE JACK BENNY PROGRAM (Episode: *Gaslight*, USA, 1952), Paula
    Alquist.
THE CHRISTOPHERS (USA, 1952), Guest Hostess.
LETTER TO LORETTA (USA, 1955), Guest Hostess.

FORD THEATRE (Episode: *Sudden Silence*, USA, 1956), Irene Frazier.

GOODYEAR THEATER (USA, 1958), Midge Varney.

ZANE GREY THEATER (USA, 1958–9), Various Characters.

THE BARBARA STANWYCK SHOW (USA, 1960–1), Hostess, Various Characters.

WAGON TRAIN (Episode: *The Maud Frazer Story*, USA, 1961), Maud Frazer.

GENERAL ELECTRIC THEATER (Episode: *Star Witness: The Lili Parrish Story*, USA, 1961), Lili Parrish.

THE JOEY BISHOP SHOW (Episode: *A Windfall for Mom*, USA, 1961).

WAGON TRAIN (Episode: *The Caroline Casteel Story*, USA, 1962), Caroline Casteel.

THE DICK POWELL SHOW (Episode: *Special Assignment*, USA, 1962), Irene Phillips.

RAWHIDE (USA, 1962), Nora Holloway.

THE UNTOUCHABLES (Episodes: *Elegy* and *Search for a Dead Man*, USA, 1962–3), Lt. Agatha 'Aggie' Stewart.

WAGON TRAIN (USA, 1963–4), Kate Crawley.

CALHOUN: COUNTY AGENT (USA, 1964), Unaired Pilot.

THE BIG VALLEY (USA, 1965–9), Victoria Barkley.

THE HOUSE THAT WOULD NOT DIE (John Llewellyn Moxey, USA, 1970), Ruth Bennett.

A TASTE OF EVIL (John Llewellyn Moxey, USA, 1971), Miriam Jennings.

THE LETTERS (Paul Krasny, Gene Nelson, USA, 1973), Geraldine Parkington.

CHARLIE'S ANGELS (Episode: *Toni's Boys*, USA, 1980), Toni.

THE THORN BIRDS (USA, 1983), Mary Carson.

DYNASTY (USA, 1985), Constance Colby Patterson.

THE COLBYS (USA, 1985–6), Constance Colby Patterson.

INDEX

Note: Page numbers in **bold** indicate detailed analysis. Those in *italic* refer to illustrations.

List of Illustrations

While considerable effort has been made to correctly identify the copyright holders, this has not been possible in all cases. We apologise for any apparent negligence and any omissions or corrections brought to our attention will be remedied in any future editions.